LESSONS:

The Craft of Acting

Truthful human
behavior on stage and screen

TOM ISBELL

MERIWETHER PUBLISHING
A division of Pioneer Drama Service, Inc.
Denver, Colorado

Meriwether Publishing
A division of Pioneer Drama Service, Inc.
PO Box 4267
Englewood, CO 80155

www.pioneerdrama.com

Editor: Arthur L. Zapel
Assistant editor: Audrey Scheck
Cover design: Jan Melvin
Cover photo by Brett Groehler, University of Minnesota Duluth
Actors pictured: Jessie Rae Johnson and Charles Gorrilla

The Library of Congress has cataloged the paperback edition as follows:

Isbell, Tom, 1957-
  Lessons : the craft of acting : truthful human behavior on stage and screen /
    by Tom Isbell.
        p. cm.
  ISBN-13: 978-1-56608-111-5 (pbk.)
  ISBN-10: 1-56608-111-4 (pbk.)
1. Acting. I. Title.
  PN2061.I78 2006
  792.02'8-dc22

                                2005032964

        1   2   3   20   21   22

To Pat

Acknowledgments

For granting me a semester leave to finish this book, I offer enormous thanks to the University of Minnesota Duluth, and in particular: Patricia Dennis, Jack Bowman, Vince Magnuson, and Chancellor Kathryn A. Martin.

I am indebted to the countless students who have inspired and taught me so much over the years, especially Adam Hummel for his specific comments regarding this particular manuscript. Thanks also to Bill Mondy for twenty-plus years worth of friendship and conversations about acting.

My sincere and appreciative gratitude to the teachers and directors who have influenced me over the years: John Ahart, Zoe Alexander, Andrei Belgrader, Michael Blakemore, James Cameron, Leslie Dektor, Wesley Fata, Earle Gister, David Hammond, David Jones, David Knight, Michael Murphy, Steve Pearson, Mark Ramont, and Lloyd Richards.

An eternal thank you to my family for their undying support from the day I first announced I wanted to be an actor. Every actor should be so fortunate.

Contents

A Definition of Acting

"Acting is the art of saying a thing on the stage as if you believed every word you utter to be as true as the eternal verities of life; it is the art of doing a thing on the stage as if the logic of the event demanded that precise act and no other; and of doing and saying the thing as spontaneously as if you were confronted with the situation in which you were acting, for the first time."

— John Barrymore

Preface

Before you purchase this book you need to know something: This is not a how-to book. If that's what you were in the market for, I strongly suggest you put the book down, step back, and walk away. I mean it. Don't waste your money. If you're looking for a how-to book on acting, *this is not it.* I'm sorry to disappoint you, and I do hate to lose a sale, but it's better if you know up front what this book is and what it isn't. It is meant to improve your acting skills; it is meant to develop your awareness as an actor — awareness both of yourself and those around you. It is meant to enlighten, to provoke, to inspire, to challenge. It is not meant to "teach you how to act."

This is not a how-to book. I abhor how-to books in the arts, especially for the theatre. Not only do they not work, but they create distance between truth and falsehood. If theatre — or any of the arts, for that matter — could be taught like paint-by-numbers, then it wouldn't be an art, would it?

Acting, especially, is one of the arts most resistant to codification. It is full of intangibles. It (seemingly) lacks the systematic exercises designed to improve one's skills. Unlike a pianist with her scales, for example, there is no true equivalent for actors. It is an ephemeral craft, with one rehearsal being completely separate from the next, one performance wildly different than the following.

Given that context, a true acting book — one geared to the emerging artist — should avoid anything resembling "how-to." Instead, such a book should focus on allowing the natural artist to evolve, grow, and mature. It should encourage the actor to find his or her own voice.

Yes, tricks can get you work every once in a while. But being an artist makes you a true actor, and true actors have a better chance of working consistently.

Don't get me wrong. How-to books do exist on some subjects: Sewing. Building birdhouses. Filing a patent. But such books don't exist for acting. They can't. Acting is learned on one's feet, either in performance or in the classroom. It is not learned through reading alone.

However.

You can greatly *enhance* your acting ability by understanding what is worth pursuing, what is worth remembering, and what is worth letting go. By reading a book such as the one you're currently holding in your hands, you can acquire *knowledge* about acting, which in itself won't land you jobs, but can strongly increase your possibilities of finding employment. By understanding and incorporating the lessons in this book you give yourself a fighting chance to work consistently as an actor, and that's all you can ask for in a business with far too many actors and far too few jobs: A fighting chance to succeed.

While it's true that books concerned with tricks on so-called "technique" can improve your chances of working as an actor, it is no coincidence that the great actors, who have no need to rely on tricks, work the most often and with the best material. I hate to burst your bubble, but despite the outlandishly high unemployment rate for actors, anyone can get work as an actor. As proof, just turn on your television any given night and flip through the channels. You're bound to see any number of actors at work.

But are they artists?

Are they creating works of any substance?

And will they last?

You and you alone know where you are as an actor. If you haven't had any acting experience but want to "make it big," this is definitely not the book for you. If you've had any actor training at all — from just an introductory level to a degree's worth of classes — and want to improve your skills, this is probably a good fit. But my feelings won't be hurt if you put this book back on the shelf and walk away. And no one need ever know you even picked it up.

This book is a series of lessons, many of which are based on a saying, an aphorism, a famous quote, sometimes even a cliché. If you like, you can think of them as mantras. Whatever. In all cases, they represent the big and little truths of acting. Learn these lessons, absorb them into your soul, *test them out on-stage*, and you will find improvement and success. Only give lip service to them and you may not be so lucky. If you're new to acting, they should provide a foundation on which you can build your acting life. If you've been acting awhile, I hope these lessons will confirm what you already know deep within you, but perhaps haven't yet voiced. The attempt here is to articulate the intangible — to capture lightning in a jar. That's what being an actor is, and that's what being an artist is.

There. You know where I'm coming from. The choice is yours.

Introduction

One more thing before we begin.

You will notice I keep things simple in this book, and that's intentional. Although it requires plenty of thinking, acting is not strictly an intellectual endeavor, so it makes no sense to confound the matter and make it harder than it is. That's why I've organized this book the way I have — to make it simple. The lessons are short (as they should be); the concepts understandable (also as they should be). It would be easy to make this book far longer than it is, but that would only complicate the issue, which, quite frankly, has gotten complicated enough, as evidenced by all the different kinds of acting books in print.

We've heard it said about other facts of life, and it's true for acting as well: keep it simple. This isn't rocket science, after all. We're not dealing with microchips or metaphysics or operating TiVo. We're talking about creating truthful human behavior on-stage. What could be more straightforward than that? The road to great acting is the road to simplicity, and I encourage you to keep your approach to acting as simple as possible. After all, this is what the great actors and actresses have discovered over time — the need to keep it simple — so why shouldn't you? If the great Spencer Tracy claimed that the key to acting was to just "know your lines and don't bump into the furniture," he must have known something about simplicity.

(By the way, because I use the word "simple" on occasion, I should point out that there is a significant difference between simple acting and simplistic acting. "Simple" is the stripping away to the essence of the thing, getting rid of the unnecessary, finding the core of the matter. "Simplistic," on the other hand, is oversimplifying the issue. It's ignoring the wonderful complexities of the issue. Taking that definition into consideration, acting should be simple, as should the *study* of acting.)

As you go through this book, you will notice a number of lessons that overlap with other lessons and that there is a certain amount of repetition. Good. That's as it should be. It would be virtually impossible to compartmentalize and pigeonhole every single aspect of acting so there would be no overlap. Besides, as an actor (and a student), I tend to pay attention when the same concepts make multiple appearances in various contexts. The great lessons bear repeating and are a fundamental part of *other* lessons, and it only makes sense that a lesson that first appears in **The Fundamentals**, for example, should re-appear (in another form) in **Classes and Rehearsals** or **Performance.** In other words, not only do I not apologize for the repetitions, I embrace them.

Lastly, before we go any further, I need to explain my definition of success, since I'll be using that word a lot. Remember, success is entirely subjective. What is successful for one person may be a disappointment for another. When I mention success in this book, I'm talking about two things and two things only: (1) being the best actor you can be, and (2) working as an actor on some kind of consistent basis. I'm not talking about income; I'm not talking about fame; I'm not talking about the cover of *People* magazine. Not that I'm discouraging any of those things if they happen to work out for you, but they don't figure into the primary definition. Improve yourself so you're the best — and most marketable — actor you can be. Create acting of unsurpassed quality. That's success. The rest will follow.

In other words, don't compare.

This is, perhaps, the biggest and most dangerous trap actors can fall into, and that's why it's imperative that your only comparisons are against yourself. The question to ask is, are you a better actor than you were in the past (last week? last month? last year?)? If so, great. If not, why not? What's holding you back? Then you can ask yourself, are you getting cast as much as you'd like to be cast? As you *should* be cast? Those, to me, are the important criteria. Not whether you've won an Academy Award (only a very small minority of actors have), nor even if you're a household name. You're a successful actor if you're the best you can be and you're working on some kind of consistent basis, whether that's in New York, Los Angeles, Minneapolis, Chicago, Wichita, Disney World, or on a cruise ship. Don't let anyone tell you differently.

Remember: Success is completely individual. It's not for us to judge someone else. We should be concerned only with our own personal success, and that's what this book strives to do. Learn the lessons, put them into practice, and succeed. Focus first and foremost on the craft. Any great artist — whether Michelangelo working as an apprentice fresco artisan or Ernest Hemingway filling his journals with writing before even attempting a novel — knows that you must first master the craft. The great artists start out as craftsmen and then continue to draw on those fundamental skills in their approach to art. To be a successful artist is to be a successful craftsman. Once you have truly mastered the craft, then you can call yourself an artist. Not until then.

A caution: There is a difference between paying lip service to your craft and mastering it. The former can be done by skimming these pages or lounging in a green room. The latter comes with age, an accumulation of life experiences, and practice. Be diligent, but also be patient. The journey is long, but when you reach the destination — the right to call yourself an artist — it will be well worth it.

There's an old saying, "All glory comes from daring to begin."

That said, are you ready to begin? Are you ready for the lessons themselves?

Andrew Bennett, Jason Peterson
Photo by Brett Groehler
University of Minnesota-Duluth

Approach

Lesson 1:
Acting Is Not Learned from Books Alone

You're feeling ripped off, aren't you? Maybe even angry. You went to the trouble and expense of buying this book, you read the Preface and the Introduction, and here I am saying that acting can't be learned from books alone. You're probably wondering if you can get your money back.

Before you throw this book against the wall, let me explain.

Remember when you were in high school and you did those annoying exercises in speech class where you played with emphasis? You know, you had a sentence like, "I didn't say that to him," and the teacher made you recite it six different times, emphasizing a different word each time?

"*I* didn't say that to him."

"I *didn't* say that to him."

"I didn't *say* that to him."

"I didn't say *that* to him."

"I didn't say that *to* him."

"I didn't say that to *him*."

It was a fun exercise, and its purpose was to demonstrate what happens when you emphasize certain words over others. Essentially, it was a line-reading exercise. Well, that's what I want you to do with the title of this lesson: Emphasize a certain word and see what happens. And the word I want you to stress is "alone."

Acting is not learned from books *alone*.

I believe very strongly that we can learn a great deal about our craft — and that's what good acting is: a *craft* — from reading. The problem arises if all we do is read and never bother to put into practice what we're learning. In other words, if it all stays in the head, in that blasted logical side of the brain, and we never try out these theories to see if they really work in practice, then there is little hope for improvement. Acting is learned on one's feet — in performances, in classes, in rehearsals, in staged readings — augmented by what we learn from books, peers, teachers, coaches, plays, films, and other actors. But we can learn so much by reading the theories and experiences of those before us, whether it's Uta Hagen, Constantine Stanislavski, Richard Boleslavsky, Sanford

Meisner, Robert Lewis, Stella Adler, Michael Shurtleff, or countless others. They have acquired so much wisdom in their own searches as artists that it only makes sense we should try to learn from them.

I know, there are some actors who say, "But I want to do it on my own. I don't want to have to learn from others. I want it all to come from me." Well, let me tell you, there's a word for actors like that: unemployed.

So. Read this book (since you've bought it, you may as well finish it). Learn from it. *And put the lessons into practice.* Try them out. Don't take my word for it; see for yourself what works when you're actually on your feet in rehearsal or in the classroom. After all, that's how you ultimately learn: through experience. Take the lessons you read here and then experience them for yourself.

That's all I'm saying. Acting is not learned from books *alone.*

Understood?

Lesson 2:
You Can Do This

I truly believe this. If you apply yourself to these lessons, if you truly examine your strengths and weaknesses as an actor and set out to correct the latter and emphasize the former, if you work untiringly to better yourself, you can work successfully as an actor. I mean it.

The problem is that you will get discouraged. Things won't always go your way. Maybe you'll have a bad day in class, or you'll give a mediocre performance, or you'll get terrible reviews, or you'll blow a big audition, and that will set you off into a spiral of depression, accompanied by all those little voices in your head that say, "See? I told you you weren't good enough."

You know what? Everyone has bad days. Everyone gets bad reviews from time to time. Everyone blows auditions. Even Laurence Olivier, considered by many to be the greatest actor of the twentieth century, once said, "No matter how well you perform, there's always somebody of intelligent opinion who thinks it's lousy." The trick is in picking yourself back up and going for it once again, this time with renewed determination. Don't let those inner voices win. The secret is to fight through them.

I know an actor who pins his worst reviews to the bulletin board in front of him. They stay up there for years. He uses them as inspiration. He doesn't keep his good reviews, which are many, just the bad ones. Those negative words inspire him to work harder, to push himself further. Bravo. That's one way to do it.

The great danger in disappointment is that it leads to inactivity; it leads to bitterness; it leads to sitting around in green rooms or diners complaining with other actors who should also be working on their craft but instead are lulled into the easy trap of *talking* about the work instead of *doing* the work. And, believe me, no one improves through talk alone, just as no one improves through reading alone. (Have I mentioned that already?)

The other factor necessary to succeed is honesty. You can do this if you are truly honest with yourself — if you admit your weaknesses as an actor and address them. It's all too easy to want to brush those weak aspects of your craft under the rug, but those are usually the very qualities that prevent you from getting cast. Be honest with yourself. Address your needs.

In his lecture on Stanislavski's method, the director and acting teacher Bobby Lewis said, "Art requires order, discipline, precision, and finish." In other words, there's work involved. You can't rely on talent alone; you have to work as well. But the good thing is *it's fun work.* Acting is exhilarating work. And the payoffs are incredible.

So get out there and go for it. Better yourself. You can do it. But only if you're honest with yourself and you work at it. One hundred fifty years ago Ralph Waldo Emerson wrote, "Nothing great was ever achieved without enthusiasm." So be enthusiastic in your striving to be the best actor you can be. That's all anyone can ask of you.

Lesson 3:
Before You Learn, You Must Unlearn

Sounds kind of Zen-like, doesn't it? You're probably afraid I'm going to go all feng shui on you. Fear not.

The truth is, we carry a lot of baggage with us as actors. So much so that the first thing we must often do is abandon the old techniques that get in the way of the new improvements. To truly make strides in bettering your acting, you must first allow yourself to change how you work.

Let's face it. Most high school acting (and I'm generalizing here) is about the joy of putting on a play. It's all "Hey, let's put on a show! My uncle has a barn and I've got a hundred Source Fours in my basement!" kind of stuff. And you know what? That's great! That's what first experiences in theatre should be about: the fun in doing a play.

But if you're seriously considering acting as a career you need to take things to another level, and one essential first step is to evaluate your past technique. My guess is that for most inexperienced actors (and here I go generalizing again), acting is a matter of learning lines and blocking. Period. That's it.

I've got news for you. If you don't know it already, acting is far more than that. It's about creating believable characters who behave in a truthful manner on-stage, as if things were happening to them for the first time. Now if you're a natural — and there are some actors out there who are — then acting really is about learning lines and blocking. But if you're like the vast majority of actors, you need to do a little more than that. There's no shame in that.

So the first thing you should do is unlearn your past mode of working and find a new way. Allow yourself to try other techniques and see what's best for you. The best actor training is a matter of picking and choosing: sampling various methodologies and choosing what works best for you. You take a little something from this teacher, a little something from that teacher, this from that book, that from this book. The goal is to create an acting amalgam that is uniquely yours: to pick and choose until you find just the right method of approaching a character that works for you. No one's feelings will be hurt if you ignore this technique for that one. The whole intention is for you to improve as an actor, whatever method you choose. So let yourself unlearn your past way of working, and allow yourself to learn new ways.

With that in mind, you're ready for the next lesson.

Lesson 4:
Know Your Enemy

There are four primary enemies that prevent successful acting. Just four. That's not so bad, is it?

And before we get too far, you need to understand that if you're going to improve as an actor, you need to know what you're up against. In other words, what's preventing you from achieving that improvement you desire as an actor? As Sun Tzu wrote in *The Art of War* over two thousand years ago, "Know your enemy and know yourself."

So what are these four enemies?

The first is **self-consciousness.** At its extreme, it manifests itself as stage fright — that inability to step on-stage in front of others and mutter even a single word. For many non-actors, this is a very real fear, which explains why the number one fear in America is public speaking (even ahead of death!). But stage fright is the extreme, when it's most noticeable, and frankly, that's not something most wannabe actors truly suffer from.

What most inexperienced actors suffer from is a less subtle version of self-consciousness which is far more hazardous, because it's not as easily detectable to a discerning audience. It is the actor so much aware of the audience that he can no longer walk "normally." He no longer knows what to do with his hands. He no longer knows how to say an ordinary sentence. Yes, this actor walks and talks on-stage, but in a manner that isn't genuinely realistic. His movements are stiff and self-conscious; his inflections are consistently downward. All too often we come to accept this self-conscious behavior as part of the "conventions of theatre," when we should demand otherwise. An actor no longer in touch with his impulses has let the enemy of self-consciousness win the battle. There is no way he or she can exist in the moment; there is no possible way such an actor can achieve genuine or truthful behavior.

The second enemy to successful acting is the deadly notion of **trying to get it right**, the subject of the next lesson. For the actor who overcomes the first enemy and thinks he's on the road to success, this second enemy is equally lethal. This notion is based on the precept that if you do step A followed by step B, you will achieve step C, which is the desired result. If only it were that easy.

If only *any* art form were that easy.

This way of thinking is also tied into the desire to please. It's the misguided notion that there is a correct way to play each and every character — that there's a right and wrong to the business of acting. This is a trap which many "over-achievers" fall into, the good students who have always excelled at whatever courses they've taken and believe (mistakenly) that the same holds true for acting. The fact is, there is no one path for good acting. It differs for each actor. As Herbert Bayard Swope said in a speech over fifty years ago, "I cannot give you the formula for success, but I can give you the formula for failure, which is — try to please everybody."

The third enemy is **self-righteousness**. For the actor who has come to believe so powerfully that her work is so good, that the show she is currently in is so brilliant, she may very well fall into the trap of self-righteousness. In this world, there is no true discovery on-stage. There is no true give-and-take with the audience. There is no genuine engagement. Rather, there is a form of preaching, where the actor becomes the most holy reverend and the audience a mere spectator. It creates a form of deadly theatre, about which Peter Brook wrote so eloquently in *The Empty Space*. The trick is to believe in yourself and the work you're doing, but to also let yourself start over each evening. If you really start in innocence each evening, then you can let the work do the talking for you, and that's as it should be.

The fourth is **cynicism**. It is practiced by those unemployed actors and actresses in the larger cities (and those un-cast actors and actresses in green rooms) who gripe about casting, their inadequate teachers, the system, the unfairness of their situation, but who do nothing but whine and moan about their present status (or lack thereof) in the theatre. What they fail to realize is that all training is inadequate one way or the other, but they're probably no worse off than anyone else; that the system stinks, but everyone is dealing with the same system, and complaining only puts you further from the place you want to be.

The only remedy for the malaise of cynicism is action. In other words, do something. Complain less, do more. Take steps.

Don't know what steps to take to defeat these four enemies? Read on. After all, that's why you bought this book.

Lesson 5:
Don't Try to Get It Right

This is a killer for inexperienced actors. Why? Because we love answers. We love directions. We love formulas. "Let's see, if I do steps 1 and 2, I will arrive at step 3. Right?"

That's how most of us were taught in schools. Multiply pi times the radius of a circle, and you'll get its circumference. Always start a paragraph with a topic sentence. The symbol for copper on the periodic table is Cu. Sonnets are composed of fourteen lines.

The problem is that acting isn't like these other subjects. It's not math or German or chemistry. It's an art. And because there are no rules in art, it's a colossal waste of time trying to "get it right." Why? *Because there is no right to get!* (Forgive me for shouting.)

Actors are forever asking, "Is this how I should do this line?" or "Is this how I should play this character?" or "Is this right?" I'm here to tell you that these questions are a waste of time. Why? *Because there is no right to get!* (Sorry.)

I hate to be the one to break it to you, but there is no right way. There is no one way to play a character, to say a line, to scan a soliloquy. There just isn't. Because acting is an art form, it is open to interpretation; it is left to you, the actor, to make choices (intelligent choices, yes, but choices nonetheless).

But we are so conditioned as human beings to think there is only one way of doing something that we fully accept that premise when it comes to acting, and nothing could be further from the truth; nothing could be more destructive. Successful acting will only happen if you're able to silence those inner voices in your head that say, "You know, that's not really the best way to do that line." Oh yeah? Says who?!? Where does that kind of thinking get you?

The problem with too many inexperienced actors is that they try to get it right when there is simply no right to get. So they end up being tentative or afraid on-stage, or, worse, not following their impulses. They have been trained over their years of going to school that there is a right and wrong way to do things. Well, yes, that's true for most subjects. *But it's not true for acting.*

There is no right way. Period.

Lee Strasberg, considered the most famous American acting teacher of the twentieth century, believed, "The actor must guard against a search for perfect solutions. Neither on the stage nor in life do we find perfect solutions."

As an actor you need to get rid of the notion of *getting it right* as soon as possible. To that end, there are even some theatre training programs — both on the undergraduate and graduate levels — that don't allow actors to be cast during their first year at their schools. Why? To break bad habits, for one. But also because once the actor is in new surroundings, he will undoubtedly feel the pressure to *get it right.* Good training programs understand the need to break that habit as soon as possible.

All of this is not to say that directors won't often guide you to *their* way of doing a line reading, but even in those circumstances you shouldn't let yourself become a robot, merely fulfilling the wishes of the director. Too many actors give incredibly mediocre performances because they're merely doing what their director told them to do. They're trying to get right what the director wanted them to do. The director may be brilliant, but if the actors haven't owned those choices for themselves, it will be an evening of deadly theatre.

If that's going to be the case, why have human beings as actors at all? Let's just do puppet shows, or better yet, get Hollywood to create theatrical performances based on computer models.

You're an actor. You're an interpretive artist. In fact, you are *the artist* who has the most connection with the audience, and in many cases you're the reason the audience came to see the play in the first place. Not to see you do something right, but to see you *interpret,* to see your character experience the highs and lows and vicissitudes of daily life. Let's face it: We know Romeo and Juliet don't get to live happily ever after. We know that Nora is going to slam the door at the end of *A Doll's House.* We know the three sisters don't make it to Moscow. (Sorry if I've spoiled any of these endings for you.) The joy of seeing these plays over and over is not because of the story itself — we know the story — but rather in seeing how these particular actors *interpret* the story, how they play their characters.

Do you think any of the great artists ever tried to get it right? Can you imagine Picasso trying to get it right? Or Faulkner? Or Chopin? Or Mozart? Or Al Pacino? Or Meryl Streep? Or Sean Penn?

Don't sell yourself short — not in performance, not in class, not in auditions. Make intelligent choices. Commit to them. But don't try to get it right. Why? Because (in unison now) *there is no right to get!*

Lesson 6:
Acting Isn't About Rules

Along the same lines as the previous lesson, I throw this one in as well to hammer home the point. Just as there is no right way, there are no rules to slavishly follow either. Sure, it's good to be heard on-stage, and it's true, there's no point facing upstage for the majority of your performance, but in general there are no rules for acting.

Why? Because acting isn't about rules. Anyone can learn rules. It is assumed you know the rules, such as they are. Just as it is assumed any good teacher knows the subject matter inside and out. But knowing the rules isn't the same as knowing how to act. Just because you have developed great diction and can speak in classic stage speech; just because you've taken Audition Techniques and know how to enter and exit an audition space and introduce your pieces; just because you've studied the Alexander Technique and have proper body alignment; these elements in themselves don't make you a better actor. They give you the *potential* to be a better actor, but only if you integrate them into your living, breathing self.

After all, I know the rules of basketball very, very well. I understand every call the official makes. I understand the significance of the three-point line, the difference between a zone and man-to-man defense, the advantages of a bounce pass over a chest pass. But this doesn't mean I'm ready for a career in the NBA. Far from it.

To paraphrase Gertrude Stein: Rules are rules are rules.

For actors — for all artists — rules are a necessary starting place, but they need to be so integrated into the actor's soul that they aren't apparent. You want to know the so-called "rules" so well that they no longer appear like rules, and it then becomes assumed that you know what to do on-stage, when to speak, when to move, when to bow for curtain call.

Beyond that, you want to avoid anything that smacks of rules. They can only hinder your work as an artist.

Lesson 7:
The Best Actors Are Dogs

One of my most influential acting teachers said the least.

He was from Romania, had penetrating eyes, wore a beret, and he not only smoked in class (allowed in the early 1980s), but he used a cigarette holder to do so. From appearance alone, he was someone we paid attention to. He said little, but when he spoke we listened. And one of his most profound lessons was also his simplest.

One day, after a particularly mediocre day of scene presentations, he got up in front of the class, flicked the ashes from his cigarette, looked at us with his piercing eyes, and said, in his halting, heavily accented English, "The best actors are dogs because they do not interrupt their lives to act. They are dog off-stage; they come on-stage, and they are dog; they exit, and they are still dog."

He inhaled on his cigarette and returned to his seat. End of lesson.

It's an incredibly simple statement. And also highly true. Haven't you seen it yourself? Actors are in the wings, conversing, laughing, being *real*, and then, *wham*, it's time for their entrance, and it's as if they'd never walked or talked before. They move like wooden soldiers and speak with all the naturalness of Al Gore.

Being a dog, on the other hand, implies a certain freedom for an artist, as well as a genuine believability. Now don't get me wrong; I'm not saying the dog is perfect. After all, it's difficult to get the dog to do the same thing on-stage each evening, and even more problematic to create a structurally interesting performance. (Not to mention speak lines of dialogue.) But. The point is that dogs don't get in the way of themselves on-stage as actors often do. They do their thing with complete focused concentration.

So why do actors have so many problems "being dog"? Why do they find it so difficult to allow their true selves to come out?

Relaxation, for one. Trust in themselves, for another.

At the moment, of course, these are only intellectual concepts, but over time, as you read this book and put the lessons into practice, the hope is that the idea of being dog will be firmly ingrained into your natural being so that being relaxed on-stage will become second nature.

That's part of the purpose of this book, and that's why this lesson is one of the first: to get you the actor to believe in yourself and to put yourself in a position where you can relax and let your true impulses come out.

To get you to be dog.

Lesson 8:
Honor the Work, Not the Teacher

One last lesson before we move on to **The Fundamentals**.

We are conditioned to please. We want to please our parents, please our teachers, please our directors. And, in the process, we end up selling ourselves short, trying to reach an ideal that may have nothing to do with reality. Yes, I hope you have an acting teacher you can trust, one who is more concerned with your own progress as an actor and not his income (or glory or ego), and one who, quite frankly, knows what he's talking about.

But even if you have the best teacher in the country, and let's pretend you do, you will fall into a terrible trap if you try to please that teacher. Why? Because you will be trying to do it his way. You will be trying to get it right. (And we all know why that doesn't work.)

In his book, *The Great Acting Teachers and their Methods*, Richard Brestoff speaks of the need to not worship the teacher, but rather, "honor the work." As an acting teacher myself, I couldn't agree more wholeheartedly. It may be flattering to have students trying to please me, but it ultimately does them no good. If we're completely honest about it, we see that pleasing a teacher is not the way to truly grow as an actor.

So who should you please? One person: yourself. Yes, accept criticism. Yes, learn from others' comments. But ultimately you are the final judge, the one person who knows your acting better than anyone else.

Set your own goals. Do your own work. Watch your own progress. Honor your progress as an actor, but please don't get hung up trying to please your teacher or director. If pleasing gets you anywhere at all it will be, at best, on a temporary basis. Honor your work, and the progress and results will be indefinite.

Jason Peterson, Andrew Bennett, David Strong,
Kathryn M. Helbacka, Carolyn Jenson, Ryan Gallagher
Photo by Brett Groehler
University of Minnesota-Duluth

The
Fundamentals

Lesson 9:
Be Where You Are

Lloyd Richards, former Dean of the Yale School of Drama and Artistic Director of the Yale Repertory Theatre, claimed that the four most important words in the theatre were "Be where you are."

That's it. The four most important words for a theatre artist were also four of the simplest words. (I told you the great theatre artists understand the importance of keeping it simple.)

Be where you are.

These words are important for actors because they apply not only to characters in a scene (allowing yourself to "be" in nineteenth century Russia or seventeenth century England or mid-twentieth century Mississippi or wherever the play takes place), but also to actors in whatever phase they're in as part of their actor training. Before the actor can begin to work on herself, she must *allow* herself to be in a place where that kind of constructive criticism takes place.

Be where you are.

If you're an inexperienced but ambitious undergrad anxious to improve so you can "make it in the real world," don't be too hard on yourself. Allow yourself to be in your early twenties, knowing that, with work, you'll get better as you grow older. After all, you've got to start somewhere. Everyone does. If you're a recent graduate from college or grad school and you've just moved to a major market, allow yourself to be at the bottom of the ladder, even if you captured all the leads back at school. If you're someone older than a traditional student and you feel like you're far, far behind students half your age, realize you bring a life experience with you that they don't. Be where you are. Not only don't beat yourself up for your "late start," but use it as an asset. If you're an actor who works occasionally but you're frustrated because you'd like to be working even more, no amount of worrying or stressing will do you any good. Be glad you're working at all. Be where you are. If you get mildly upset every time you read the trade magazines and see the lists of *other actors* getting cast, don't read the trades. It's that simple. Be where you are.

Accept your place in the actor's journey. Work hard to improve your talents, yes, but accept your place.

In other words, in terms of your life as an actor: Don't compare. And in terms of your life as a character: allow. All summed up very neatly in those four simple words.

Be where you are.

Lesson 10:
Own It

If your attention span can't take four words as a mantra, how about we divide that number in half. Lloyd Richards has his four most important words for the actor; these are my *two* most important words: Own it.

Own everything you do. Own every move you make on-stage, every gesture, every step, every look, every glance, every nod. Own everything you say. Own every single word that comes from your mouth, every sound, every grunt, every mumble, every stutter.

Own it all. Have complete ownership of everything you do on the stage.

Why? Because you do in real life, so why shouldn't your characters have the same privilege?

Think about it. You're sitting in a classroom. How do you sit? Do you slouch? Do you cross your legs? Do you lean on the desk in front of you? Do you sit up straight? It doesn't matter. What does matter is that you inherently and instinctively own everything you do, as do all your peers around you. It's only when actors get on-stage that some of those movements seem false. Don't let them.

Instead, own them.

Think about the words that come from your mouth. Those are *your* words. First of all, you had the *impulse* to say them. Secondly, you *discovered* them. And lastly, you *spoke* them. They were your words all the way, from inception to execution. No one questions where you got those words. Through years of talking you have created ownership for how and what you speak, and so the words you say as a character should be treated with no less respect. Find the impulse for those words. Discover them. Own them as they pass through your lips.

The problem is that actors are all too often content with just *reciting* what is written on the page. I've got news for you. That's not acting. It's, well, reciting. And I've got more news for you. Anyone can recite. Anyone. It takes an artist to interpret. The best and surest way to ensure that you are acting and not reciting is to find ownership of all you say on-stage.

And where does that ownership begin? Not just on the stage, but in the rehearsal hall. Even in the classroom. I had a speech teacher who, when we were going through the tedious process of sentence drills, would stop us and ask, "Do you mean it?" Even though it was just a speech class and we were focusing on sample sentences to learn classic stage speech, she wouldn't let us get in the habit of saying words we didn't mean. In other words, she made sure we *owned everything we said*. What a wonderful teacher she was! All too often I see young actors content to just go through the process of saying words. Never let yourself just say words. Never let yourself just recite. Always own, own, own.

And as for blocking, remember: Anyone can go where a director tells them to go — a trained seal can go where a director tells it to go — but it's the true actor who makes it look like it was his idea to go there. The best actor makes every bit of blocking look like it came from the actor himself *at that very moment*. There was no director necessary (it should appear) because the actor is so connected with everything he's saying and doing.

It doesn't matter where the ideas come from; it can be the director, the director's assistant, the actor, the actor's mother. (Don't laugh; actors' mothers have had notoriously good ideas throughout the years.) The point is, the actor is the one responsible for creating ownership so that he is as believable on-stage as he is in real life.

Lesson 11:
Engage

I told you Lloyd Richards's four most important words in the theatre ("Be where you are"), and *my* two most important ("Own it"), but what if we had to distill it all down to just one word? If we had to define the single most important word for an actor, what would it be?

For me, it's simple. *Engage.*

That's what acting is: engaging. Engaging with the other performers on-stage. Engaging with the audience. Engaging with the message of the play and the style of the production. Nothing is more frustrating to me than a slick, well-oiled production where everyone is going exactly where they're supposed to be going and doing what they're supposed to be doing, but no one is connecting with anyone else or with the play itself. They're certainly not connecting with the audience. What's the missing piece? Engagement.

No matter how brilliant the blocking, the choreography, the line readings, the takes, the bits, the "moments," if there is not true engagement you are cheating yourself and cheating your audience.

That's not to say actors don't get away with non-engagement. All too often they do. A couple of years ago I saw a touring production of one of the big-name musicals (I won't mention which one), and because my wife and I arrived at the theatre just minutes before the play began, I didn't get a chance to read the playbill ahead of time. What was interesting to figure out, merely from the performances, was who had been on the tour a long time, and who was relatively new. At one extreme was an actor who had been doing this national tour for eleven years. (Eleven years of the same production!) His performance was slick, well-timed, well-executed, but shallow, shallow, shallow. That's not to say he didn't fool a large part of the audience into liking him — his was the lead comic role, after all — but for anyone knowledgeable about theatre, it was clear he was just going through the motions, not bothering to engage his fellow actors or the sold-out audience.

In contrast to him was an actress who had been on the tour less than a month. She brought a vitality and spark to her role that was refreshing, exhilarating, *engaging.* Her performance wasn't as slick as Mr. Eleven Years, but it had an honesty and depth that made her the truer actor, the truer artist. (She also got the biggest ovation at curtain call.) Even now, as I think back on that production, it is she whom I remember most clearly, not the actor who phoned it in.

Make genuine, honest contact with your fellow actors and with your audience. Don't *show* that you're making that contact, just genuinely make it. Good things will follow.

Lesson 12:
The Curse of Acting Is Acting

These were the words spoken by Charles Jehlinger, the famed acting teacher and creative head of the American Academy of Dramatic Arts. He even took it one step further and went on to say, "Good actors don't act. Bad actors act. Good actors create."

"Acting" is showing the seams; it's letting the wires show; it's giving away the tricks. As an audience, we can't truly lose ourselves in a play if we're too aware of the actors at work. There is no suspension of disbelief, willing or otherwise, because we don't feel like we're watching characters, but rather *actors*. It's an important distinction.

Effective acting — acting of a kind that seems effortless and honest — should not feel like acting. It should feel real; it should be genuine. It should feel like a real conversation, a real argument, or a real love scene. It shouldn't be *acted*; it should just, well, *be*. As the rhetorician Quintilian said back in the first century, "The perfection of art is to conceal art." In other words, don't act.

Okay, I admit: Easier said than done. So how do you get to this place where you're not *acting*?

Simple. Read on.

Lesson 13:
Follow Impulses

Even though you just purchased this book and I hardly know you, I'm going to make a blanket generalization. (Are you sitting down?) Here goes. All of you holding this book were brilliant actors when you were young. All of you. Brilliant actors.

There. I've said it. Pretty brash statement, isn't it? But I'm right, aren't I?

And how do I know this?

I know this because I do know you. I know all kids. I know that we have an innate sense of fun as children, that we're drawn to play, and that we don't interfere with play when we're young as we do when we're older. Far from it. We give ourselves over to the activity or the game, never once hesitating to think about the "rightness" or "wrongness" of what we're doing.

I remember playing war in my parents' front yard. (This was in the early sixties, mind you, when there was nothing the least bit un-p.c. about playing war.) My friends and I would point our plastic rifles at one another, say "Bang, you're dead," the victim would fall to the ground, count to ten, and come up firing. I have a distinct memory of falling into the snow-covered honeysuckle, rolling down the embankment, landing at the bottom, counting as quickly as I could, and springing to my feet, ready to take out the Nazis (the other neighborhood kids) who had killed me.

And you know what? I wasn't half bad. As a World War II soldier, I had some things going for me. Why? Because there were no voices in my head telling me I couldn't do it. There were no internal critics saying, "You know, you're really not right for this role. After all, you're too short. That's a plastic rifle you're holding. And you're only six years old."

There was none of that, and as a result, I had complete commitment to my work. I believed in what I was doing. I didn't for a moment second-guess any of my choices.

I didn't think, I just did. I was trusting my instincts. I was following my impulses.

I'm sure you, too, had your own games, such as *Star Wars,* or house, or Dungeons & Dragons. Whatever. The point is, we were all brilliant actors as kids.

31

But look at us now. We're on-stage, either in rehearsal or performance, and we have an impulse to do something as simple as put a hand in a pocket, or cross our arms, or walk from here to there, and yet some blasted internal voice says, "You know, I'm not sure your character would do that." So we start the move, and then, halfway through, we cut the impulse and stop the motion entirely.

What happened? Well, over the years we learned etiquette and manners that are appropriate and necessary to live in a civilized society (not bad things in themselves; they just happen to be death to actors), and we have smothered our wonderful true impulses under layers and layers of "appropriate behavior."

You can see the results of all that layering with inexperienced actors. They desperately want to cross from stage right to stage left, for example, and you can see them *leaning* in that direction — sometimes to the point where they're listing more than the Titanic — but some voice has gotten in the way of their impulses and they're afraid to follow through. Or they're sitting down and they start to cross their legs, and then, *bang*, halfway through the move they stop, their leg dangling in air like some levitation act. We have a world full of young, twitching actors — actors who begin to follow an impulse and then chicken out halfway through.

So what's the solution? How do we get back to that pure place where we can follow our impulses and fall inot the honeysuckle?

Like an onion, peel away all the outer layers. You've got to get to that place where you're able, once again, to *recognize* those impulses, and then, even more importantly, to *follow* them. It's a two-step process. That's the only hope you have for truly being in the moment. Don't think. Just do. Don't concern yourself with what's right or not, with what's appropriate or inappropriate. That's what directors and teachers are for. They'll let you know if you're making a choice that's not consistent with the rest of the play or even with your character as a whole. But they can't truly make those decisions until they see a living, breathing human being on the stage, one who trusts himself enough to follow impulses.

Let yourself go. Allow it to happen. In acting classes, silence those inner voices, trust those instincts you have and go with them. See what it's like to be a child again. Peel away the layers.

Use rehearsals as a place to find out whether your character is the type to put his hands in his pockets, or fold his arms, or cross his legs. Try it. See how it feels. See if your director says anything to you. If it feels good and your director doesn't have a problem with it, put it in your character's repertoire. It's an acceptable gesture, and maybe you'll use it in the show and maybe you won't, but you'll know it's there. Yes, there is such a thing as an incorrect instinct; you may have an impulse that isn't appropriate for that play. That's why you want to be in a place as an actor where you're comfortable enough to follow your impulses *in rehearsal* so you (and the director) can determine if they're the most appropriate choices for that production.

The problem with most inexperienced actors is that they don't use rehearsals wisely enough. They don't use them as place to follow their impulses and see where those impulses take them, and so they get to performance and they're still not sure what exactly they "should or should not do" (terrible words for an actor, by the way).

Get in the habit now of finding the child in you and following those impulses. And get in the habit of testing out those impulses in rehearsal, so you can determine (before opening night!) what's appropriate for your character and what isn't.

In other words: Get back to the honeysuckle and counting to ten and believe in yourself on-stage.

Lesson 14:
Want, Want, Want

I had so much fun making that sweeping generalization in the previous lesson I'm going to do it again.

For my money, there's no more important aspect of acting than motivation. If you take nothing else from this book, take this: *You must always, always, always want something on-stage.*

Always?

Yes, always!

In other words, "What do I (as my character) want?"

"What do I want in my life?"

"What do I want through the course of this play?"

"What do I want in this scene?"

"What do I want *at this very moment*?"

What is a want? It's the same as an objective. An intention. A motivation. A *desire*.

Why are wants so important? Because (prepare yourself for another sweeping generalization) we have them every single waking minute of our lives.

We no longer articulate them to ourselves, of course, because our brains are working in a kind of shorthand, and there's no need for an inner monologue to say, "Let's see, I'm hungry. Therefore, I'll make myself a piece of toast. But to accomplish that, first I need to walk into the kitchen. Then I'll remove a slice of bread from the bag. After that, I'll take it to the toaster. Of course, I'll need to plug in the toaster. Once I've done that I can place the bread in the toaster." You get the picture.

Instead, there is some unpronounced impulse from stomach to brain, and before we know it, we're interrupting what we were previously doing and walking to the kitchen to prepare the toast.

The point is, we always want something. That's why we do the things we do. If we didn't have objectives — if we didn't want anything — we'd just collapse on the ground. We *want* things. Even in our most couch potato-like states in front of the television, we want something. (In such situations, the intention is usually "to relax.")

You want something right now in reading this, otherwise you wouldn't be reading it. Your objective may be to learn, it may be to understand, it may be to get a job, it may be to pass an exam for school for which this is the text. There could be any number of reasons why you're going through these pages right now.

The point is, you always want something. Always. And your characters do as well. Therefore, never let yourself be on-stage without an objective. Never, never, never, never, never.

Think of scenes as battles. You want something. Your scene partner wants something else (usually in opposition). The stage is your battlefield. And the two of you skirmish over who will get what they want. That's what makes the scene interesting and gives it life: the fact that each of you wants something different from the other.

You know the old saying, "It's better to give than to receive"? I hate to break it to you, but in acting it's just the opposite. As a character in a play, you want, and it's far more important that you get than that you give. There are precious few altruistic characters in plays (they tend to make for boring drama); the overwhelming majority of characters desperately want something, and they'll often go to any lengths to get it. Good. That's dramatic. That makes for interesting theatre.

So the other big question to ask yourself, then, is "What's in my way? What's preventing me from getting what I want?" Because there's always an *obstacle*. (More on that two lessons from now.) If there were no obstacle — if there were nothing standing between you and your objective — there would be no conflict, and without conflict, there is no drama. And all well-written scenes have that dramatic conflict.

Imagine a scene about a first date. We've all been there, right? Your objective usually is to see if you like the other person, and, perhaps more importantly, to see if the other person likes you. What's the obstacle? You don't know this person yet. You don't know her values, her history, her sense of humor (if she has one). These are all things you need to find out. And in terms of her liking you, that's what you need to find out, too. Does she laugh at your jokes? Does she appreciate your stories from childhood? Does she act interested when you tell her about your work? All this information and knowledge is exchanged because each of you has an objective. A strong and *playable* objective.

But, of course, just deciding on an objective isn't enough. You need to play it. You need to try to get it. It does no good if the objective stays in your head. *It needs to be played.*

There are several keys to wants that will make you a stronger and more interesting actor.

1. Define your objective in terms of what you want *from someone else on-stage.* Wanting world peace is an admirable desire, but it's not a very playable objective. You want something that will get you involved in the scene, and what better way than by wanting something from your scene partner? *Always want something from someone else on-stage.* The only exceptions are if it's a monologue, in which case you want something from an imaginary off-stage person, or a Shakespearean soliloquy, in which case the objective is usually to either figure something out or come to terms with something.

2. Keep objectives active. Even in the most mundane situations, find a way to make your objective strong, present, *active.* Lloyd Richards used to say that even in situations such as being at a bus stop on-stage, you're not *waiting* for the bus; rather, you're *catching* the bus, which merely hasn't come yet. The difference, which may strike you as minuscule or even silly, can make all the difference between doing *something* or *nothing* on-stage, and *something* is always preferred.

3. Keep your objectives positive. (I'm not speaking morally here.) If, for example, your objective as Richard III is to seduce Lady Anne, whose husband and father-in-law you have just killed, that is a perfectly acceptable choice. (In fact, "to seduce" is always a strong and playable objective.) Returning to the first date scenario, your objective will probably be along the lines of, "I want her to like me," as opposed to "I don't want her to hate me." The first is positive; the latter is negative. Approaching objectives from a negative angle will only make you weak, and though there are certainly characters who think in these terms, try to keep your character's objectives positive.

4. Be able to state your objective clearly and succinctly. If I stop a scene and ask an actor his objective at a particular moment and his reply is a rambling, multi-sentence treatise, I know he won't be able to play it. You can't play it if you can't define it simply. Practice phrasing your objectives in one sentence. "I want her to like me." "I want to convince him I didn't steal the money." "I want to make her feel guilty." Any longer and you will be stuck in the head and not playing impulses.

Where and when do you make decisions about objectives? In rehearsal. In the classroom. Write the objectives in the margins of your script (in pencil) and test them out. If an objective doesn't work, erase it. Try something else. That's what rehearsals are for: Testing objectives and learning to trust impulses.

And do you know another time to make sure you're playing

objectives? In auditions. The vast majority of film and TV auditions, for instance, are scheduled only twenty-four hours in advance. You'll have barely more than an afternoon and evening to pick up the sides, read through the scene(s), and *make decisions about the character and what you want.* In most cases, you won't have access to the full script, and even though you may not completely understand everything that's happening, if you can choose objectives and honestly pursue them, you will be interesting in that audition room. Whether you're what the producer and director are looking for is another matter, but that's out of your hands anyway, so why worry about it?

Let me repeat that: If you can choose and honestly pursue objectives in an audition situation, you will be far ahead of the great majority of actors out there.

Do all actors write their objectives in the margins of their scripts? When Robert DeNiro works on a film, does he pencil in his motivations next to his lines? I seriously doubt it. But when you've reached his high level of competency as an actor, you're able to make shortcuts. You begin to think that way automatically, and you don't need to go to the trouble of writing them down. But my guess is that if you're reading this book you're not at that place just yet. In other words, go ahead: Write your objectives in the margins. Then use the rehearsal process to try them out. When you're a more accomplished actor, you can use shortcuts.

One last point. There's no shame in playing a character who doesn't achieve his objective. In fact, if you study the great plays, you'll notice that the most memorable characters don't get what they want. Romeo and Juliet don't get to live happily ever after. Cyrano doesn't marry Roxanne. Willy Loman doesn't succeed as a salesman. That's part of the reason they're great characters: they're interesting and complex and trying desperately to adapt to what they're given. But rarely do the great characters get what they want.

Now that you've figured out what wants are — and you know you always need to want something on-stage — you need to know how to achieve those wants. Which leads us, rather conveniently, to the next lesson.

Lesson 15:
Play Actions

If an objective is "What do I want?" an action is "What do I do to get what I want?" Very simple, yes?

Let's return to the first date scenario. If you have defined your motivation as, "I want this other person to like me," then what do you do to achieve that? You compliment her. You pay for dinner. You open doors for her. You act interested in her stories. Perhaps you make her laugh (or try to). Maybe you tell her how multi-talented you are. Whatever. The point is, you *do things* to get what you want. And you keep making adjustments to the scheme. If this action doesn't work, you try another. If that one doesn't work, you try another still.

It's not enough to merely articulate your objective; you're going to have to break things down and work step-by-step. You're going to have to *find tactics* to get what you want. You're going to have to play actions.

For instance, you want this other person to like you, so suppose you try to achieve that by first impressing her with your knowledge of fine wines (this is Tactic A in your quest of your objective). The waiter shows up and you speak fluent French and nonchalantly rattle off names and years as casually as if you were discussing a grocery list. Of course, unknown to you, your date doesn't drink and couldn't care less that you're a spirit aficionado. All you realize is that Tactic A didn't have the desired effect, so you go to Tactic B.

Tactic B is to show her what a marvelous sense of humor you have. You try out some of your best material, offhandedly talking about a funny incident at the office and still ... Nothing. No response.

So, on to Tactic C. You'll show her how smart you are. You mention your undergraduate GPA, your numerous graduate school degrees, your startlingly high IQ, but even this doesn't have the desired effect.

Tactic D. You prove to her you're a SNAG (Sensitive New-Age Guy). You recite your favorite passage from *Leaves of Grass* and get teary-eyed halfway through it. You try to go on, but the emotions overwhelm you. Glancing up through your fingers, you see your date is not impressed. Therefore ...

Tactic E. Etc., etc.

Being a character in a scene is a matter of making adjustments from Tactic A to Tactic B to Tactic C to Tactic Infinity, doing whatever it takes to get what you want.

Remember: A scene is a series of battles. If you don't win, you keep changing tactics — changing *actions* — until you make headway. You're still playing the same overall objective; it's just that you need to alter your actions throughout the scene because the current actions aren't getting you anywhere. You need to do something different to get what you want. Or, if a particular action *does* work, then you up the stakes, switching to a new tactic to try to get even more.

I have a friend who was on one of the *Star Trek* shows, and she said her greatest difficulty was finding new actions to play each week, because her character went through such similar ordeals. Finally what she did was to buy the biggest thesaurus she could find, and she went through her script each week and intentionally chose different active verbs for her actions so that her performance would be different from week to week. She wasn't content to play the same things over and over; she wanted to continue to stretch as an actor. She wanted to make sure she was doing something different.

And that's the key: *doing*. Acting is about doing, and that is no more apparent than in the playing of actions. After all, at its core, theatre is based on action.

Lesson 16:
Find the Obstacles

There is always an obstacle. If there weren't, there would be no conflict. If there were no conflict, there would be no drama. Curtain. End of show. Goodnight, everybody. Tip your waitress on the way out.

There is always an obstacle. If, in the first date scenario, Boy likes Girl, Girl likes Boy, and there are no obstacles, it will be a short, unsatisfying scene:

Act I

(A BOY and GIRL are discovered eating dinner at a
    fancy restaurant.)

BOY: You know, I really like you.

GIRL: That's funny, because I really like you. (They lean in
    to kiss each other. Slow fade to black.)

End of Play

See? It's not all that interesting. There needs to be something in the way. There needs to be an obstacle. For instance:

Maybe Boy likes Girl, but Girl isn't so sure she likes Boy. Boy's objective, then, is to *persuade* Girl that she should like him. And Girl's objective is to *discover* whether she likes Boy or not. That's playable, that's interesting, and there's a conflict.

Or maybe Boy likes Girl, Girl likes Boy, but Girl just got out of a long-term relationship and isn't sure she wants to get involved again. That's an obstacle, even though it's an internal obstacle. So she must *determine* if she likes Boy enough to make herself vulnerable to another relationship.

Or maybe Boy likes Girl and Girl likes Boy, but they got off to a bad start (the premise of many a romantic comedy), and one of the two must *persuade* the other that they're right for each other.

There can be any number of reasons why these two will have to struggle before they get together, because if they get together too soon, what's the conflict? That's why, in most romantic comedies, the couple doesn't get together until the very end. Why not earlier? Because there are too many obstacles in their way. And if they do get together too soon, there is no more conflict. There is no more sexual tension.

Playwrights — good ones, at any rate — know that scenes are

based on conflict, so that whatever it is your character wants, there's a good bet that another character on-stage wants something in opposition to your want.

Maybe Boy has difficulty talking to beautiful women.

Maybe Girl doesn't laugh at Boy's jokes.

Maybe Boy's car broke down, and he was late picking Girl up, and she is still irked.

Maybe Girl hates this restaurant.

Maybe Girl doesn't think Boy is funny.

Maybe Girl sees that Boy has spinach in his teeth.

Whatever. These are all obstacles.

Sometimes these obstacles are given by the playwright, sometimes by the director, and sometimes the actor needs to invent them herself. In this way you're not only finding obstacles, you're also *creating* obstacles.

One simple way to make scenes interesting is to place obstacles in front of your scene partner. If you're certain you know what he wants, make it difficult for him to achieve it. If you know he wants your eye contact, have your character look away. Make him work for it. If you know he wants you to agree with him, walk away. Make him earn it. And if you're in rehearsals for a play, don't be afraid to change your reactions to what he's doing. It'll force him to pay attention and stay in the scene, as well as make him work harder to get what he wants.

You can also give yourself obstacles. As actors, we tend to be enormously lazy about our choices. If we see that the character would have a pencil in the scene, we usually have it handy and at our disposal. But why? Isn't it true that whenever you really need a pencil in real life you can never find one? So why not do the same to your characters on-stage?

Or, say you're playing a lawyer, and your line to your law partner is, "But wait a minute, wasn't he convicted five years ago of a felony?" There are no stage directions with the line. Just that line, presumably said to the only other person on-stage, the law partner. Instead of just saying the line, why not make it difficult for yourself? Why not, halfway through the line, realize you can't remember when this person was convicted, or of what, and so you have to get up and find a legal pad and flip through it until you come to the information you want. The line will now read, "But wait a minute," (the actor rises, crosses to his desk, finds a legal pad, flips through it, his fingers dancing down the margin until he slaps the paper, finding what he wants), "wasn't he convicted five years ago of a felony?"

All of a sudden, you have given your character another dimension. He is a real person who forgets and needs to find things. He makes a discovery on-stage, as opposed to just knowing everything beforehand. And how did you accomplish all this with one single line? By providing an obstacle for yourself.

Now, granted, you don't want to do this for every line, but you need to always be on the lookout for such opportunities. They're not gimmicky; they're real life.

In other words: Hunt for the pencil, turn the sleeve inside out, misplace your glasses, find lint on your sweater. The more of this you make yourself do, the more you'll find yourself naturally doing, the more you'll be *in the moment*.

Find the obstacles. I guarantee you, they're there. And your acting will be all the better for it.

Lesson 17:
Discover the Subtext

Now that you understand objectives, you'll be tempted to race through the script after first reading it, writing in the margins all of your character's wants based on what they're saying.

Be careful.

In the good plays, intentions aren't so readily apparent. The characters don't always speak the truth. Why? Because *we* don't always speak the truth. We don't go running around spouting our objectives, articulating what we really want. At college parties you don't go up to the beautiful co-ed and say, "Hey, I think you're really good-looking, and I'm attracted to you. What say we leave this place and go to my apartment?" That may be what you're thinking, but you don't dare come right out and say it. Instead, we ask where she's from or what her major is, as if you care about any of that. But you ask those questions, and you carry on that dialogue with the subtext heavy in your minds.

As interesting as a society might be if everyone went around saying what they really felt, that's simply not how we conduct our everyday lives. Good playwrights know this, and their plays are heavy with subtext. It's not always what the actors are saying that's interesting; it's what's *beneath* the words.

I'm convinced one of the most powerful scenes ever written in the English language is Scene Five from Harold Pinter's *Betrayal*. The couple, Robert and Emma, is in Venice on vacation, having a conversation about where they'll visit the next day (Torcello), what book Emma's reading, a little talk about the publisher, the agent, the author. On the surface it seems like a nothing scene.

But what they're really talking about is something completely different. After seeing a letter the day before written to Emma from Robert's best friend Jerry, Robert is wondering whether his wife is having an affair. His objective in the scene is to find out if his suspicions are correct. Thus, questions about Torcello (where he and his wife honeymooned ten years earlier) have a double significance. The same with talk about the book. Jerry is a literary agent and represents this particular author, so Robert's asking about the book is another way of needling Emma. Emma's objective at the beginning of the scene might to be figure out why Robert is behaving so oddly, but as the scene progresses her objective naturally changes to "Does he know?" A very playable objective indeed. Later it changes to "How much does he know?"

It's a brilliantly written scene, with all the good stuff underneath the lines. On the surface it may seem trivial, perhaps even banal. But it's the *subtext* that makes the scene go, that makes it one of the most powerful scenes written in the twentieth century.

Do all plays have such subtext? The good ones do. That's what makes bad soap operas so frustrating to watch for many theatre people. There is very little subtext. The lines give everything away, and even if the lines don't, the actors often do, as if to make sure the audience gets it. How boring and uninteresting is that?

In the theatre — as in real life — it's the subtext that makes things interesting. It's what is going on underneath that is compelling. The words are mere tips of massive icebergs.

Lesson 18:
What Do the Other Characters Want?

Now that you know to always want something on-stage, there's another element to add as well: What do the other characters want?

I hate to be the bearer of bad news, but it's not enough to only know your own character's intentions, you need to determine the other characters' intentions as well. I'm not talking about going up to the other actors on break and asking them (far from it!); I'm talking about trying to figure out during the course of the scene what they're trying to get from you.

Why on earth would you bother to do this?

Again, because this is what we do in real life. As we're in the midst of interactions with other people, we try to figure out what they're after, because goodness knows they (like us) rarely come right out and ask for it. So not only are we pursuing our own wants, but we're also pursuing the additional want of trying to figure out *their* wants. (Got that?) Then, if we like the person and are in the right mood, we'll agree to help him out, but if we don't care for the person or we're not in the mood, we'll create more obstacles for what he wants. Returning to the college party scenario, if the beautiful co-ed determines that the guy talking to her is actually hitting on her, and she's not attracted to him, her intention suddenly changes to repel his advances. Maybe she'll say she needs to go to the bathroom. Maybe she'll invent a fictitious boyfriend who's a starting linebacker for the football team. Maybe she'll claim she'll be busy washing her hair for the next month so he shouldn't bother calling. But she resorts to these tactics only when she has discovered what he truly wants. Up until then, it might have been a perfectly nice conversation.

I'm not suggesting that determining the other characters' intentions should be your primary point of focus in a scene, but it should be an element that you do address, if only because (1) it's true to life, and (2) it will keep you from anticipating on-stage. The more you're genuinely discovering things on-stage for a first time, the more likely that your responses will be truthful and in the moment.

One other aspect about this lesson. You might figure out another character's objectives the first week of rehearsal, but please, please, please don't assume his objective will remain the same throughout the remainder of the rehearsal process, or even during the run of the show. If he's any kind of serious actor, there's a good chance that he, like you, will be experimenting with different objectives, trying to find the ones most suitable for his circumstances. So by all means, try to determine his intentions, and then stay in tune with how his choices change throughout. It will make you all the more aware and engaged on-stage, and that, after all, is half the battle.

Lesson 19:
For Heaven's Sake, Do Something

I remember my first year doing summer stock. I had just finished my freshman year in college, I knew next to nothing about acting, and I somehow found myself in a summer company doing a repertory of four plays, none of which I was terribly good in. One night after rehearsal, the director was racing through his pages and pages of notes, giving each of us various adjustments to make before the next rehearsal. At one point he stopped and looked up from his clipboard, staring me straight in the eyes.

"What are you doing at the top of Act II?" he barked.

I thought a moment. "I'm just standing there. I'm not doing anything."

"Wrong answer! For heaven's sake, do something." And he went on with his notes.

It was a lesson I never forgot.

Do you realize that at every waking moment we're always doing something? Even in a classroom, listening to a teacher lecture on and on, we're doodling with a pencil or playing with our gum or passing notes or counting light bulbs or trying to get someone's attention. We never stop. Even when we lie down at home to get comfortable, we're usually nibbling on a snack, or rubbing our feet, or glancing over the sports pages, or flipping through the channels on the remote or examining the latest CD. *We're always in motion.* And remember that people are defined more by what they *do* than by what they *say*. That's Playwriting 101, and it's Acting 101 as well. (That's why the great acting teacher Sanford Meisner had the following maxim framed and hanging in his classroom: "An Ounce of BEHAVIOR is Worth a Pound of WORDS.")

So why do actors suddenly stop everything when they get on-stage? Why do they just sit there, or stand there, or put their hands in their pockets? Why don't they do anything?!? Because they've started "acting" and stopped living. Stopped being. No longer existing in the moment, they are content to stand around and wait for their line.

But that's not what we do in real life!

There are two ways to approach this problem, and they are the two ways to approach most any acting problem. One is the outer

47

way: by examining the consequences and consciously making changes and adjustments so that by force of habit you'll begin to engage yourself in activities. In other words, begin to invent things to do on-stage.

The other approach is the inner way: Through the cause. The cause of this lack of activity is simple: The actor is not truly being in the moment. If he were, he would be doing something. Right? Okay, that's clear enough. So, how to fix it?

Simple. By *allowing*. By giving yourself permission to be there.

How many times have you seen it happen? A director stops a scene and shares some thoughts with the actors on what they're doing. The actors gradually let down the trappings of their characters and soon are sitting on their feet, fiddling with their beards, running their hands through their hair, picking at the tear in their blue jeans ... whatever. The point is, *they're doing something*. They're being. They're allowing themselves to be in this place, which in turn allows them to *do something*. And you know what? They're *interesting*.

So what happens as soon as the director walks away and says, "Let's take it from the top of the scene"? The actors stop what they're doing, they sit up straight like robots, they stare into each other's eyes like characters from *Night of the Living Dead* and cease to be *real human beings*. They've stopped being, and therefore they've stopped doing. Granted, there are roles where it would be inappropriate to pick at your blue jeans or run your hand through your hair (most any Ibsen play, for example), but I would rather see actors making alive choices and letting real human behavior exist on-stage (even if it's inappropriate) than see non-humans reciting memorized lines.

Of course, the ultimate goal is to combine the two and make alive choices and be appropriate all at once, but I wouldn't worry about "appropriate" early on. There's plenty of time for that. Besides, I don't know of a single respected director who wouldn't gladly prefer real human behavior on-stage; it then becomes his/her job to lead the actor to more appropriate choices. That's no big deal.

Another way to break out of the non-activity habit is through very external and obvious means: Do activities. With any scene you do, find whatever props can be there for you and start dealing with them. Is it a scene that takes place in a living room? Great. Then there will be magazines on the coffee table, perhaps framed family photos, lamps with light switches, little knickknacks, and any other number of objects that will exist for your "doing pleasure." Is the scene a kitchen? Even better. There's food to be had from the fridge, a toaster, a teakettle, a microwave, a skillet, dishes to put away, counters to clean. It's an endless list. Make a choice! Do something! Don't be put off just because the script may not mention anything about eating or drinking; unless it's an O'Neill play, there's never room in any script to list all those kinds of details. And although there will be plays where it might be "inappropriate" to butter a piece of toast while the other character is talking about the death of a loved one, it might not be inappropriate to be absent-mindedly playing with a spoon, or a salt shaker, or a napkin.

I worked with an actor in television who works fairly steadily in series and movies-of-the-week. He's no Laurence Olivier, but one thing he does do is find activities. He's always rustling through folders, jotting notes on legal pads, playing with phone cords; and it gives the appearance of another dimension to his character. There's no reason why you can't do the same. If you're in a play, make choices, try them out in rehearsals, see how they feel, see what the director says, try other choices, don't give up. Keep finding something to do. If you're in front of the camera, bug the prop person — that's what they're there for, after all. And although they may be amazed that this new actor on the set is asking for these props, they will come to respect you for using them. (A rarely known secret in the TV and Film Industry: Every person on the set wants to feel used. They want to feel a part of the whole. So engage them!) And the director, who rarely has much time for supporting actors in television, will love you for breathing life into your character, which in turn breathes life into the finished project.

Some directors and teachers refer to this as "tasking." Fine. Whatever name you give it, it's up to you to flesh out your character and find those things to do that your character would do. Please don't wait for the director or teacher to give you ideas; find them for yourselves.

The bottom line is: *Think!* Be creative. Find something to do and then do it. If you stop and really analyze your day-to-day life, you'll see how much you actually do. Don't sell your characters short by not doing an equal amount yourself. For heaven's sake, do something!

Lesson 20:
Personalize Everything

I have refrained from mentioning this earlier because I was afraid once you read this lesson you would quit reading. But do you want to know the two essential ingredients to successful acting? Conquer these two elements and I guarantee you will work consistently as an actor.

1. **Truthfully want something on-stage.** (Not just "want something," but "*truthfully* want something.")

And the second key ingredient?

2. **Personalize everything.** That's it. It's that simple. So what, you ask, do I mean by personalize?

I mean for you to make everything you *do* on-stage as an actor — every glance, every gesture, every cross, every bit of body language — and everything you *say* on-stage — every word, every sigh, every grunt and mumble — come from someplace real, from someplace *personal*.

Think about it. Every word that comes from our mouths in our daily lives is so uniquely and utterly *ours*. We own those words; we thought of them; we uttered them. We're never reciting. Those words mean something to us. Otherwise, we wouldn't say them. There's an *attitude* to each and every word we say.

So why do we allow ourselves to say things on-stage that seem completely foreign to us? Because we haven't personalized. We haven't made those words our own. We haven't allowed ourselves the opportunity to find a point of view for what we're saying, which will in turn shape *how* we're saying it.

How do you go about personalizing? In a couple of ways. You can always use substitutions. In other words, draw from experiences in your own past which relate to the character's. Let's say you're doing a play in which your character's father dies, but in real life both of your parents are still alive, so maybe in your mind's eye you substitute a favorite grandmother for your character's father and that creates a believable on-stage experience for you. Or maybe you employ Stanislavski's "Magic If," thrusting yourself into the experience so completely that the on-stage events are real for you, in which case you don't need a substitution because you truly will be moved by the events around you.

Whatever method you choose — and remember, there is no "right" way — you need to make sure that you have personalized the acts and words of your character. It's not a robot you're playing (unless, of course, you're playing a robot); it's a breathing, living, reacting human being. So let her be specific and real.

Look around you. With luck, you're reading this in a place where there are other people present. Notice them. See how they're standing, or sitting, or walking. Each person has found a unique gesture, or posture, or a way of holding her pencil or twirling her hair. No two are alike. And yet, as actors, we tend to iron out the distinguishing qualities of our characters, making them utterly bland. Why? Because we haven't personalized.

Too often actors find themselves in situations where they're just saying words. The playwright has given them an emotional speech, but the actor either rushes through it or glosses over it. And yet nothing could be further from real life. When, in our daily lives, we have those moments where we speak of things that matter to us (the subject of most plays, yes?), each word we say is charged with our own personal stamp. Our own highly personal point of view. We're not just talking to talk; we're speaking from the heart. These are the times that playwrights have chosen for their plays: The heightened moments in our lives. So it is a mistake to just rattle off words (or gestures or blocking or body language) as if you're neutral. I've got advice for you: Characters aren't neutral!

One more point about personalization. Oftentimes in rehearsal a director will say your character needs "more levels." What is the normal actor's response to this all-too-common comment? He or she begins to wildly create various qualities, many of which are random, all for the sake of creating variety. A better and more truthful means to create levels is through more specific personalization. Remember, we have differing feelings about the different things we do and say, so of course it only makes sense that by being more specific in our personalization we will in turn create the differences (or levels) that the director rightly wants.

Personalize the material. Personalize every physical thing you do on-stage and every word you say on-stage. We do as actual human beings. Why shouldn't we as actors?

Lesson 21:
Experience, Don't Show

Of all the bad habits that inexperienced actors carry with them, none is more aggravating (or detrimental to truthful behavior on-stage) as feeling the need to indicate to the audience. For some unknown reason inexperienced actors feel compelled to *show* the audience that it's cold, that they're out to kill the other guy, that they're lying, that they're in a hurry. And yet, in reality, when we find ourselves in these situations (well, I can't speak to the killing one), we try to do anything but show. We usually try to cover up.

The single best advice I can give young actors is to *experience,* don't *show.* Try to genuinely find what it's like to be cold, or in a hurry, or angry, or in love, or sad, and *experience* those sensations. Then the work will take care of itself. The performance will take care of itself. Your facial reactions will be perfect, your gestures just right. But if you feel the strange need to *show* the audience all these things that your character is experiencing, you will come off as transparent, two-dimensional, unbelievable, and false. (I hope I didn't sugar-coat it.)

Part of the problem lies with stage directions. In parentheses, right before the line, is the word "gloomily" (or "angrily" or "soothingly"), and so we feel compelled to act gloomily (or angrily or soothingly), whatever that may mean. Stage directions are merely clues. They are hints. They are there to guide us along. *They are not there as rules to be slavishly followed.* (If you need a reminder about this, consult Lesson 6.)

Uta Hagen, in her bible of a book, *Respect for Acting,* suggests actors cross out all the stage directions of the plays they're in. And there is a certain sense to that. But I don't mind stage directions as little hints, given to the actor from the playwright herself. As long as I don't get stuck trying to *show* those qualities to an audience, I should be okay. The trap occurs when I feel like the audience must know everything I'm experiencing. Why that's dangerous and false is because that's not at all reflective of truthful human behavior. In real life we don't go around showing that we're cold; instead we do some small thing (keeping our hands in our pockets, for instance, or continually wiping our runny nose) that may, to the insightful spectator, demonstrate we're cold. But it's not something we're committed to showing others.

And remember, you can't play states of being anyway.

One of the most common mistakes actors make occurs when their character lies to another character. For whatever reason, inexperienced actors feel this strange need to make sure *we get it*, so they overplay the lie. They indicate to the audience. As a result, they become completely unbelievable, when in fact, in real life, most of us are pretty good liars. If I'm in a scene and the script calls for me to lie to another character, I want to be such a good liar that the audience — like the other character — won't know if I'm lying or not. The last thing I want to do is telegraph my intentions.

So experience these emotions and sensations, and trust that if you are genuinely connected to them, they will play appropriately for an audience.

Lesson 22:
Talk and Listen

Every art has its basics; every sport has its fundamentals. For the pianist, it's playing scales. For the painter, it's drawing. For the basketball player, it's dribbling, passing, shooting.

What is it for the actor? Two things: Talking and listening.

Look, we can make acting far more complicated than it need be, but it really comes down to these two elements: The ability to talk and listen realistically on-stage. Do those two things, and at least you'll be believable as an actor on-stage, which, after all, is the goal.

So why is it so difficult to talk and listen as actors? I mean, we don't seem to have any trouble doing either of those on a daily basis. But on-stage we often forget to listen altogether, and our talking can sound more like recitation than genuine conversation. Talking is something we do naturally enough on our own, goodness knows, but given memorized text, we suddenly become robots, not resembling human life at all.

The main problem is that, through the rehearsal process, we have come to know everything we say and also everything the other people on-stage will say. As a result, we *anticipate*. There's no need to really listen, we think, because we know what they're going to say. And there's no need to really talk, because somehow we have kidded ourselves into thinking that "the lines will take care of themselves." Yeah, right.

It's fashionable to talk of the brain being divided into two sections — a logical side and a creative side — and although scientists now claim this is somewhat simplistic (there are actually more than just two), it's helpful in terms of thinking about successful talking and listening. When we're genuinely talking and listening, we're working out of that lovely creative side; when we're reciting memorized lines and pretending to hear words that we know are coming, we work from the dreaded logical side.

So how do we overcome these difficulties?

Let's deal with talking first. The primary reason talking on-stage sounds so false is because actors aren't really talking (duh!). *They aren't actively playing an objective.* They're not trying to convince their scene partner of something, or persuade them, or get something from them. The actor may have intellectually identified the want, but she's not actively playing it. She's not using the words as we use words in our daily lives: As ammunition. She's merely *saying* the words, an act which bears no resemblance to talking at all. The best way to make sure your talking is real is to remind yourself of the objective and go for it. Use the words (and the silences and the physicalities) to *get what you want*.

And trick yourself. Don't assume you know the outcome of the play. Pretend that this rehearsal, this performance, things might be different. You might just be so convincing in your talking that the author's words will change and the other character will agree to what you want. Wouldn't that be something?

One clear sign that actors aren't really talking is when you hear them excessively using downward inflections as they speak on-stage. If, in real life, you're telling a story, your inflections continue to rise because you want to make sure the person to whom you're talking knows the story is continuing. You only resort to downward inflections at the ends of major thoughts or at the conclusion of the story itself. And yet all the time on-stage you hear actors lapsing into downward inflections because they're reciting the lines from that hated logical side of the brain. If we're really talking, we don't use downward inflections nearly as much.

How can you fix the downward inflection problem? Once again, internally or externally, your choice. The external solution is to simply be aware of the problem and not let yourself lapse into the downward inflections except for the appropriate times. It's one more thing to think about, but if that's okay with you — and *if it works* — then by all means go for it. The internal solution, which I prefer, is to make sure you're genuinely trying to communicate, you're genuinely trying to achieve your objective. Do that, and the talking will take care of itself, and the inappropriate inflections will disappear.

Problem solved.

Listening is, in some ways, more difficult, but only because we make it so. In reality, there is nothing easier than listening, but on-stage we work so hard at *showing* we're listening that we forget to really listen. And it doesn't help that for four weeks you have been hearing these same words from your scene partner, and now, in performance, you must act like you're hearing them for the first time. That's the problem right there. You're thinking about "acting" like you're hearing. You mustn't do that because that will lead to a showy performance; it will lead to indicating. As the great acting teacher Charles Jehlinger said, "Listening is listening; it is not acting that you are listening." He even went on to claim that "the whole basis of acting is listening." Pretty strong words for such a simple activity.

So how do you make it happen on-stage?

Trick yourself. *Allow* yourself to hear these words for a first time. Remember that even though you don't have any lines when you're listening, that doesn't mean your character isn't alive and active and thinking. So as you're listening, make sure you have a strong objective that you're trying to achieve. Again, don't feel the need to *show* that objective to an audience, but make sure you experience it for yourself.

That will lead to genuine, active listening on-stage, which is always far easier than we choose to make it.

Lesson 23:
Take Stage

One final lesson before stepping into the classroom or rehearsal.

There is no place in theatre or film for the tentative actor. You may be shy in real life — and I've known some terrific actors who are *painfully* shy on a personal level — but when it comes time to step on that stage, you need to be fearless. You need to be bold. You need to take stage.

Oftentimes the performance we're drawn to is not the actor who creates the character with the most nuances, it's the actor who is the boldest, who is the most unafraid to stand on that stage and say, "*Look at me.*" Whether we want to admit it or not, it's that kind of bravura that grabs our attention. It's that kind of confidence we respond to.

Don't stand around waiting for permission or for someone to give you praise. Take stage. If you've done the work, you should have no problem committing to your choices, and you shouldn't be shy about sharing those choices with an audience.

Be bold. Be brave. Take stage. You — and the audience — deserve no less.

Annie Ragsdale, Andy Frye, Tom Isbell
Photo by Brett Groehler
University of Minnesota-Duluth

Classes and Rehearsals

Lesson 24:
"You Are Only As Good As You Dare Be Bad"

Ah, paradoxes. I love them.

Have you ever seen this quote? Back in the 1970s, the Academy of Dramatic Arts used to run full-page ads in various theatre magazines with a handsome picture of Robert Redford and the words "You are only as good as you dare be bad" suspended above his head. Another way of putting it, as stated by Jim Keating, is: "Dare to suck."

Whichever quotation speaks to you, you need to know that as an actor the only way you can truly stretch yourself and extend your boundaries is by willing to fail, by trying different things night after night in rehearsal with the hope that even a tiny fraction of those choices will work. You need to let yourself be bad on a regular basis, and from those choices you can stick with the few that actually work, and work well.

It's important that all actors recognize this essential fact, because otherwise your co-stars will wonder why you're making the choices you're making during the rehearsal process, while they, by contrast, have found something that works okay for them in an early rehearsal and they're willing to stick with it forever. There's no growth in that kind of actor. Making the same safe choices over and over again does not interest me as an audience member, and it certainly doesn't interest me as a fellow actor.

Be willing to take risks, to make outlandish choices, to be bad. Because you'll learn more about yourself — and your character — by allowing yourself that process. Dare to suck.

Of course, it helps if you have a director who understands this process, and, truth be told, there are far too many directors who don't have that kind of trust in actors and who panic whenever they see a "bad choice." It's a pity that such directors exist, but, of course, they do. Does that mean you should change your process and play it safe? Absolutely not. Will it make it harder for you to truly let yourself "be bad" in such situations? Undoubtedly.

But for your own sake as an artist, let yourself grow, experiment, change. Challenge yourself. Think of the great artists, from Mozart, to Picasso, to Faulkner. What made them great was their willingness to try new forms, to experiment, to push themselves past acceptable or so-called "safe" choices.

If you truly wish to be an artist of the theatre, that is your only choice as well. Allow failure. After all, we tend to learn more from our failures than our successes anyway. As Robert F. Kennedy once said, "Only those who dare to fail greatly can ever achieve greatly."

So fail. Suck. Be bad. In the long run, you'll be all the better for it.

Lesson 25:
Don't Play for the Blue Pen

Huh? What blue pen? Did I miss something here?

Let me explain.

I am partial to blue pens. I have scores of them. Whenever I teach a class or direct a play, I can be found scribbling away with my blue pen, taking copious notes that the actors know they will soon receive. And an interesting thing happens, especially with inexperienced actors; they begin to model their performances based on my notes. They begin to play it safe, desperately hoping I won't write down a note for them with my dreaded blue pen.

This is a terrible mistake.

To begin with, I'm just another person in the theatre. While I may have a certain amount of experience as a teacher and actor, it is a shame when young, highly talented actors stifle their impulses because of any notes I — or any teacher or director — might happen to be writing. (The ironic thing is that often my notes are positive, and it's actually a *good* thing to get a note, but of course actors only remember the "bad" notes. As someone once said, it takes forty positive notes to outdo one negative one.) I'm not saying you should disregard what a teacher or director has to say to you, but I am saying you should do your work fully and wholeheartedly. There's plenty of time to take in notes and make adjustments later. If you're constantly playing for the blue pen, you're never going to give yourself a chance to experiment, to play, to explore.

Forget the blue pen. Forget the fact that there's someone taking notes. Forget the fact that someone's even watching you. Rehearsals are for you, and the only true way you can use them to your best advantage is if you tune out all outside distractions — including the scratching of certain blue pens — and focus on what you need to focus on in the scene, which, usually, is your scene partner. Then, when the scene is over, you're ready to listen to notes from someone who has the advantage of being a neutral — and informed — outside observer. But when you're in the scene, you want nothing that will stand in your way of focusing on your objectives, your scene partner, your personalizations, your talking and listening, and everything else that goes into a well-acted scene.

Play for yourself, your fellow actors, your audience, but not the blue pens of the world.

Lesson 26:
Read the Play, Not Your Part

Tell me if this sounds familiar. You've been cast in a role, and you're reading the script for a first time. What's the first thing you do? If you're like most actors, you race through it to see how big your part is. You may do this by just skimming through the pages until you see your character's name. Or, only slightly better, you may actually "read" the play, but every time you come to your character's lines you say them out loud, even though this is your first encounter with the script. (This is known as the "yadda, yadda, MY LINE, yadda, yadda, MY LINE" method of play reading.) I encourage you to avoid either of these methods.

When you are cast in a play there is little of more importance than your first reading of the play. That first reading, when you're approaching the play with innocent eyes, will give you your first true taste of the style of the play, what works in the play, and the play's effectiveness on an audience (an audience, at this point, of one). You will never get another opportunity to have a fresh reading of the play, so it's vitally important that you stay true to it. Don't skip to your lines. Don't read your lines out loud. Approach the play objectively, as an audience member does, and you will get more from it. Goodness knows you will have plenty of time to say the words out loud; a first reading is not that time.

One of the pitfalls actors make when they do a mini-performance with their first reading is that they create line readings. They jump to choices that are based on no research whatsoever, and because these choices are drilled into the head early on, they are the toughest ones to break.

Approach the play purely. Give it a fair read. See how it all fits together and what emotional responses you have to it. Let it wash over you. Let the themes present themselves to you. Let the climaxes speak for themselves. Don't take notes. Don't highlight. (Again, there's plenty of time for all of that later on.) Just read and enjoy and savor.

The work can come later.

Lesson 27:
Practice Good Rehearsal Habits

If you want to be treated (and cast) like a pro, then you need to behave like one. And a true actor understands what's expected from rehearsal:

Be on time.

Come prepared.

Learn your lines.

Carry a pencil.

Don't goof around.

These are all self-explanatory, of course, but please know that if you consistently break one or more of these conditions, your director will notice. And directors not only have long memories, but directors talk. The chances are good that if one director knows about your work habits, *many* directors will know about your work habits.

In addition, there are some more subtle nuances of rehearsal you should know as well. For instance, *never give another actor notes.* That's not your job. That's what the director is being paid for. If you don't like something another actor is doing, figure out why you don't like it. Is it because it bothers you personally, or is it because it would bother your character? There's a difference. If it's you personally, you'll just have to get over it. If it's the character, then you need to find a way to *use* what the other person is giving you. Think of it as an obstacle and be grateful, because obstacles can only help your performance.

Be sensitive to the process of other actors. Each person has her own style, and you need to be aware of how she works so you don't interfere with her process. The trick is to focus so intently on your own goals that others will want to work with you again. You concentrate on your own rehearsal process and make sure your own work habits are good, and everything else will take care of itself.

Trust me.

Lesson 28:
First In, Last Out

In sports, there's a concept known as FILO: First In, Last Out. It refers to the mentality of athletes at practice, and the better the athlete, the more time he will spend working at his discipline. In other words, the truly committed athletes are the first ones to arrive at practice and the last ones to leave.

There are innumerable examples of this very concept, whether it's the legendary shortstop Ozzie Smith taking extra fielding practice every single day, Larry Bird shooting an extra one hundred free throws, or wide receiver Jerry Rice staying after practice to catch even more passes from his quarterback. In each case, the extra time spent at their craft made all the difference between their being good athletes and being great athletes.

Actors should demand the same high standards from themselves.

It's all too easy to kid yourself into thinking that "now that you finally know how to act," all you need do is learn your lines, show up at rehearsal, put forth a modicum of effort, and everything will fall into place. Or so you think. This is especially true for actors who are seniors in college, or in their third year at graduate school, or who have been in the real world for a while. If things have gone their way and they're not careful, they can get lazy.

But the far more interesting actor is the one who continues to arrive early to warm up and go over lines with other cast members, and then stays late to pick the director's brain long after everyone else has left. That's the actor who is interested in improving. That's the actor directors want to cast.

Arrive early. Do a little warm up. Stretch your physical boundaries so that at each class and at each rehearsal you will be able to push yourself just that much further. Don't be one of those actors who arrive at rehearsal at the last moment (or *late*). Don't be one of those acting students who come to class and are all too happy to get comfortable in their chairs, *waiting* for class to begin, *waiting* for the teacher to tell them what to do. Take the initiative. Do something on your own. Run lines. Do a monologue. Warm up. *Take stage.*

Be the first one to arrive at class and rehearsal, and be the last to leave. Remember that it is the greatest privilege to be an actor, and you should savor every moment of it, making it last for as long as you can. If you're the first to arrive and the last to leave, not only will you extend your acting time, but you'll enrich your time as an actor. You'll find improvement. You'll raise the level of the actors around you. You'll earn the respect of teachers. Directors will want to cast you.

The more you think about it, it seems like a pretty easy choice. First in. Last out.

Lesson 29:
Show Up

The actor who is present — in class, in rehearsals, at auditions — is the actor who is giving himself a fighting chance. The actor who prefers to stay home (or at least stay away from class, rehearsals, and auditions) is the actor without work.

As Woody Allen put it, "Eighty percent of success is showing up." And it's true.

Show up. Be present. Go to class even when you don't feel like it. Make the audition, even though you don't think you have any chance of getting the part. Not only go to rehearsal, but give it your all, even if you (mistakenly) think you've figured it all out.

Show up. Be present.

I can't tell you the number of times I got cast professionally when I thought I had no chance of getting the job. But I showed up anyway and good things happened. I can't tell you how many classes and rehearsals ended beneficially, even though I might have dreaded going. That's what showing up does for you.

And don't think people don't know when you do and don't show up. As an acting teacher, I'm very aware of who's hungry, of who has the desire, of who's really putting forth the effort. It's the ones who show up. And not only do they show up, but they're ready to work, which means they're ready to play, which means they're ready to be cast.

Show up. Be present. Even — and especially — when you don't feel like it. That's when the glory comes.

Lesson 30:
Be in the Moment

You know how in the *Star Wars* movies Yoda is always saying "Trust the force"? Even when Yoda is not present, we hear it as a kind of dreamy voice-over. "Trust the force, Luke. Trust the force." Well, the acting equivalent is "Be in the moment."

It's a phrase you hear bandied about a good deal in the theatre, and I've already used it a good deal so far. "Such-and-such actor is so good; she's always in the moment." "I didn't believe you in the play; you weren't in the moment."

So what on earth does this phrase mean, anyway?

Quite simply, it means believing in your surroundings and circumstances so much on-stage that the audience believes them too. To be in the moment is to *experience* what your character is experiencing, to feel what he's feeling. It's nothing that can be shown to an audience; it's nothing demonstrated. It's total belief in what's happening on-stage. It's being present.

How do you achieve it? Simple. By doing the proper kind of work *ahead of time*; understanding your character's circumstances inside and out, choosing objectives, pursuing actions, personalizing, particularizing — all elements addressed in this book. By working properly, you give yourself a wonderful chance to believe completely in what's happening to you on-stage, so that when another character says a certain line, it will bring about an emotion in you that just comes naturally.

Needless to say, there is no better feeling for an actor than to truly be in the moment.

Two words of caution: When I say you believe completely in the circumstances on-stage, I am exaggerating slightly. Truth be told, I don't think you should ever lose complete sight of the fact that you have an audience and that you're performing the play for an audience. So when I say you have total belief in what's happening on-stage, I'm probably speaking more in the 95% range. Some small part of you wants to remind yourself that you are an actor and you are in a play, just so you don't get too carried away with the events on-stage. It's always a bummer when the actress playing Juliet gets so swept up that she actually stabs herself. Kind of puts a damper on an evening of theatre.

Secondly, as you begin to grow as an actor, it will be tempting to want to scream and shout after a particularly good performance that you really felt it, that you were genuinely in the moment. Be careful of this. What often happens for inexperienced actors is that they do, indeed, find some truth on-stage, but then they become so enamored with that feeling that they throw out all the other elements (wants, actions, circumstances, etc.) and wallow in "feeling it." The best actors know it's a balance. You still need to define wants. You still need to be cognizant of circumstances. You still need to pursue actions. It's just that now you're experiencing these things more truthfully.

One last warning. There might be occasions where you truly felt in the moment and yet the director didn't believe it. The reason for this is twofold: Either the director simply wants you to go another way with the material, which is an appropriate request, or else you may have *thought* you were genuinely experiencing, but you were merely *showing* that you were experiencing. Sound confusing? Let me give an example. I have seen actors leave the stage and talk about how they were "really sobbing up there," and I look at them and want to say, "No, if you were really sobbing up there you wouldn't be able to talk. There'd be tears running down your cheeks. You'd have trouble catching your breath. You'd be, well, sobbing." Many times actors *think* they're experiencing true emotion on-stage, but instead, they're merely experiencing an indication of emotion. You need to remain honest with yourself as you begin this kind of exploration.

Like so many elements, being in the moment comes from the proper kind of work beforehand and then *allowing* yourself to live in the scene. It's that simple, really. And believe me, once you begin to experience it, you'll never settle for anything less from yourself.

Lesson 31:
The Danger of Being Careful

Nothing kills truthful acting faster and more effectively than being careful. As we live our day-to-day lives, we're anything but careful. We're ourselves, following impulses. In fact, those times when we are careful (dinner at the boss's house, for example) are usually the least successful moments of our lives.

So why do so many actors get careful on-stage? Probably fear, for one thing. Fear of playing the wrong objective, fear of not being believable, fear of not getting the laugh. What's ironic is that when we're careful, we're not really giving ourselves much of a chance to be successful at all, for we strip ourselves of the ability to follow impulses and we're too overly concerned with how we're coming off. In short, we're thinking too much about the result and not about the cause that gets us there.

We don't go to the theatre or the movies to see careful actors. On the contrary, we go to see someone bold, audacious, sure of themselves. That's what's exciting. Look at Johnny Depp. Compare *Pirates of the Caribbean* with *Blow* with *The Legend of Sleepy Hollow*. He is anything but careful. If we wanted to see someone careful we'd just look in a mirror.

Another reason why so many actors are careful is because they're still unsure if what they're playing is "correct." There are a couple of faults with this line of thinking. One is in believing there is, indeed, a correct way to play a character (Remember: *There is no right way!*), and the other is that this type of thinking demonstrates that the actor didn't test all this out in rehearsals to come up with the answers before opening night. Rehearsals are about testing everything there possibly is about the character, so that when opening night comes you have total confidence in every aspect of your character's life. Performances for audiences shouldn't be exercises in being careful; they should be celebrations of all the hard work you've done during the rehearsal process. (The problem is that far too many actors don't push themselves hard enough during the rehearsal process and wait, instead, to make those grand discoveries during the run of the play. This should be avoided for any number of reasons.)

Do the work during the rehearsal process so that, come opening night, you can play. At that point, there should be nothing careful whatsoever about your work on-stage. The same holds true for an audition. Really put forth an effort to figure out the character and scene(s) so that when it's time for the audition, you can allow yourself to play and follow impulses. There should be nothing careful about your work at all.

Time after time I see actors getting cast, not because they're the best actors in the world, but because in callback situations they're the least careful. They go for it. And that's what every actor should do.

Being careful is death. Have I made myself clear?

Lesson 32:
Give Yourself Permission

If you look up the word "permit" in the dictionary, you'll notice that at its Latin base, the second half of the word translates "to let go." As you've no doubt discovered, the best actors know how to let go — they know how to find that release on-stage — and tied in with the previous lesson of not being careful is the ability to give yourself permission, to let yourself go. I see so many young actors who don't realize their full potential as actors merely because they don't permit themselves to let go. They don't give themselves permission.

I see it in actors with real ability who are afraid to make the commitment to become actors — and given the unemployment statistics, I can't blame them — and I see it with actors on-stage simply afraid or unable to give themselves permission to fully commit to an action, to a gesture, to a choice.

And what's holding them back? They're simply unable to give themselves permission. Well, if you don't give yourself permission, who's going to do it?

I'm convinced that much of this stems from our reliance on outside approval. As I wrote earlier, we're so conditioned to pleasing parents, teachers, directors, that we're nearly unable to make — and then follow through — on choices unless we have someone's permission. It's as if we're afraid to make a choice or take a stand unless we're given permission that that's the right choice or stand to make.

But look around at the great actors (or any great artist, for that matter). What we admire about them is their audacity, their ability to go for it. Who's giving them permission? *They* are. At some point in their lives — maybe early, maybe later — they came to terms with this notion and began living their lives the way they wanted to live them. They gave themselves permission. They gave themselves permission to be actors (a good place to start), and they gave themselves permission on-stage to follow what impulses they wanted to follow and to make whatever choices they wanted to make. To their credit, they stopped waiting for the external forces to say, "It's okay. You can do this now." They took the bull by the horns and followed their heart. And by giving themselves that kind of permission, they became the artists that we know them to be.

Only you can give yourself permission as an actor. So what are you waiting for?

Lesson 33:
Be Aware

Back in the 1960s, it was not uncommon to hear people say things like, "Hey man, groove out. You're working too hard. You gotta stop and smell the roses. Otherwise, you're not hip. Dig?" Okay, maybe people didn't talk exactly like that, but they certainly did say, "You gotta stop and smell the roses," a good deal. That was one of the popular mantras from that decade.

Believe it or not, the best artists know this lesson. They are attuned to the world around them. They take in everything they can, using all their senses. A walk in the park isn't just a walk in the park; it's a chance to explore sensory details: What do they see, touch, taste, hear, and smell? Consciously or subconsciously, the best artists stop and smell the roses.

An actor needs awareness on-stage. Although most characters may not be terribly aware of their surroundings, actors need to be completely aware of what others are giving them. They need to be in tune with their senses so that nothing is passed by, nothing is glossed over. It is the actor who generalizes and muddles through the play who gives a forgettable performance. But take your time, be aware of the characters around you, and you will make discoveries that will aid you in the playing of your own character. You will find nuances that will make the play worth watching.

Actors need to be aware of other actors or else they will fall into the trap of anticipating. In the middle of a rehearsal process, test your awareness. Make sure you're really in tune with what the other actors are doing, and not just making assumptions based on earlier rehearsals. Be aware of the choices the other actors are making and how they're executing those choices. Take it in. React specifically.

Actors need to be aware of the audience, too. What is the audience giving? After all, that is the most significant difference between theatre and film: the actor/audience relationship. It's a pity when stage actors don't take advantage of this, when they just plow through the material as if it were an empty house. This is obviously true for comedies, but it's equally true for drama as well. A good actor can sense how the audience is responding and use that to his advantage.

Good actors are aware outside of the theatre as well. In fact, that's a prime place to make discoveries by being aware of the people and places surrounding you. As you're walking in a mall, perhaps you can people-watch and find the way someone walks or talks or gestures that you can use for a character of your own. Or as you're watching the sunset and are aware of the orange and purple colors that paint your surroundings, you can re-experience that feeling for yourself on-stage at an appropriate moment.

Because Helen Keller was both blind and deaf she had to rely on her other senses, and it was said that she could hold a radio and listen to a symphony concert, able to discern which instruments were playing and when. Her sense of touch was that keen. A person merely had to walk by, and by catching a whiff of his scent, she was able to determine his line of work. Her sense of smell was that acute. Now that's awareness!

The good actor doesn't blindly stumble through life. The good actor is entirely aware of everyone and everything around him, both on-stage and off. Creating such awareness for yourself is one of the easiest tasks you can accomplish in theatre. All it takes is for you to stop and see, smell, hear, taste, feel. Take it in. Process it. You'll find you're more aware than you ever thought you could be.

As Lee Strasberg said, "The actor is an instrument that pays attention."

Exactly.

Lesson 34:
Be Specific

When I was in the fifth grade I had four best friends. They were each different, and I did different things with them, but they were each a best friend. Greg was my adventurous friend. John was my funny friend. Conrad was my intellectual friend (if that's possible in the fifth grade). And David was my fishing friend. They were all "best friends" — perfectly acceptable to have more than one best friend back in grade school — but my relationship to each couldn't have been more different.

Just as you must personalize every word you say and every gesture you make, so must you be specific about everyone and everything around you. In other words, make sure everything is as real for your character on-stage as everything is real for you in your personal life.

Think about it. You have a very definite relationship with every person around you, every object around you, and every place that you're in. The characters you play deserve no less.

For example, think of your friends now. You have a very distinct relationship with each of them. You may call each of them your friend, but you use them (and they use you) differently. There are some friends who are good to laugh with. Some friends you share your closest secrets with. Some friends are fun to hang out with. Some friends you know better than others. And yet, you may call all of these people your friends.

So if you're handed a script and the stage directions tell you that you're friends with another character, determine to what level the two of you are friends, and what that means in this particular instance. All too often actors settle for easy answers. "Oh, we're friends," they say, after reading the script. "I know what friends are." And yet they don't delve deeply enough to determine just how specific that particular relationship is.

Be specific.

The same holds true for places. Think about the various places — the rooms — that you visit in a given day. Now think about your specific relationship to each. You have a different relationship with a space when you first move into it. That changes once you've lived there awhile. Same with work spaces. It's very interesting to watch students over time as their relationship changes to an acting classroom, for example. At first they're excited to be in the space; they feel like they're part of a secret club. But three years and multiple classes later, they have a far more indifferent attitude toward that space, which makes sense. After all, they might very well feel like they live in that room.

Being specific informs our on-stage life.

Think of the objects in our life and how we feel about those objects. Now why can't we make our onstage objects so specific to us?

For example, let's say you've been given a play and in a particular scene you're wooing a woman. It's your first date, she's over at your house, you've just had dinner, you're relaxing in your living room, and you ask if she'd like coffee. Yes, she says, she'd love some. So you go to the kitchen to prepare said coffee, all the while talking to this beautiful woman, and you reach for a coffee mug from the cabinet. You stop, stare at it absently, and put it back, grabbing another mug instead. What just happened?

Well, maybe your character was married before, and maybe his wife died in a tragic automobile accident. He's just now getting back to dating, and this is the first woman who has seriously interested him. The evening has been going great, and now they're getting ready to have coffee, and as the man reaches for a coffee mug he accidentally grabs one that he and his wife purchased. Together. On their honeymoon. He stares briefly at the mug, suddenly remembering his wife, then slides it back into the cabinet, not allowing himself to think of her on this particular evening.

By creating those kinds of specific circumstances, the actor has added another dimension to his character. He has added a level of history and realism which will make the character come to life. The audience may not suddenly whisper to each other, "Oh, I bet that was a coffee mug he and his wife bought together on their honeymoon," but they will understand that they are watching real, human behavior. And that's the goal.

The more you make everyone and everything specific around you, the more grounded you will be, the more interesting you will be to watch, and the more likely you will be to achieve genuine behavior.

Lesson 35:
Learn All Them Lines

It's an old joke for actors. You have just finished the performance of your life. You found every nuance possible. You breathed new life into a classic character. You are feeling the rush of adrenaline and accomplishment for having achieved the impossible. You are in the midst of removing your makeup, accepting the congratulations of family and friends, when someone (usually a distant uncle who has not seen the-*ate*-er before) comes up, takes your hand, and utters the predictable: "That was really good. How'd you memorize all them lines?"

Instead of feeling like an artist, you suddenly feel like a freak — someone capable of extended memorization, as if that was what made you successful.

Why does this happen? Because acting is a profession witnessed by anyone who watches TV, anyone who goes to the theatre, anyone who rents movies. In short, nearly everyone. And because people have such a long history of watching acting, they all have their opinions. Nothing wrong with that. What's tough is that they have little knowledge to back it up.

I have some bad news. There's nothing to be done about this. There will always be the uninformed who will offer their opinions on your acting, and all you can do is smile and nod your head. The sooner you accept this, the better.

But guess what? Believe it or not, there is actually some very real value in what your Uncle Cletus has to say. Actors have gotten so used to being in plays that, all too often, they put off the actual learning of lines. "I'll get them," they say, rather smugly. "I'll know them when it counts."

But in too many cases it's not soon enough. Why? *Because you can't really begin to work on a character until you know your lines inside and out, backwards and forwards.* Until that moment, you're stuck in the logical side of the brain, and it's the creative side where the good stuff happens. Actors are all too willing to gradually learn the lines, as if by osmosis, rather than just buckle down and learn them early on. But you know what? *You can't really begin to work on a character until you know your lines inside and out, backwards and forwards.* (Is there an echo in here?)

Know this: The sooner you learn the lines, the sooner you can play. The better you know the lines, the more comfortable you'll be on-stage. And notice I use the word "learn" instead of "memorize." That's because "memorize" implies that darn logical portion of the brain again, while "learn" suggests you know these lines with your whole body, your whole being. They are not mere words you've committed to memory; rather, they are a part of you. They are necessary for you to use these particular words to get what you want. They are your life ammunition.

How you learn them is important as well. It's not enough to sit at the kitchen table and go over them again and again. You need to say them out loud. You need to let them play on your lips. You need to create some *muscle memory* with these words. And you need to get up and move. If you sit in one place to learn your lines you're more likely to learn them by rote, to create set line-readings, and no one wants that.

Instead, why not walk around as you're learning the lines? Why not play with how you say the lines as you learn them, not choosing any one or definitive way of delivering them, but experimenting with the line readings? Why not allow yourself to gesture as you learn the lines? In that way, you'll be killing two birds with one stone: not only learning the lines but also finding a repertoire of movements for your character.

If you just barely know the lines, your performance won't be much more than a recitation exercise, lacking human depth and nuance. But learn the lines so you can say them in your sleep, and suddenly you'll be able to toy with line readings and use rehearsals properly: As a place to test objectives and experiment with actions. In this way, when it comes time for performance, you'll have the appearance of a person saying words truthfully as opposed to saying memorized lines. But if you're stuck trying to think of lines, you'll be stuck as an actor, and your performance will have as much nuance and interest as a circus performer.

Learn the lines. Learn them *quickly*. Learn them accurately. And learn them until they are a part of you.

Lesson 36:
Thou Shalt Have No Fear of Commitment

Having talked of objectives and actions, having mentioned activities, there's one thing left: To *commit* to those choices. There's no point in making choices if you don't commit to them and commit to them completely. If, when thinking of your character, you come up with a bold new way of playing a scene, there's only one way to test out the appropriateness of that choice: By committing to it fully in rehearsal. Don't waffle. Don't try to play a little of this and a little of that. Don't kid yourself that you'll commit to it in performance. Commit to it *now*. Play the one thing you've decided to play, and play it completely. Play it to the hilt. See how it feels. See how the director responds. It might not be right, but you won't know unless you try it out.

I can't emphasize this enough: There are no bad choices, there are no bad choices, there are no bad choices. Wait, no, I take that back. There is one bad choice: That is to make no choice. That's a bad choice, but it's the only one.

Nothing frustrates me more than actors who can't decide if a character is more this or more that, and so end up playing it safe and going for something in the middle of the road. Then, when they get into performance, they realize they never fully committed and hope the audience won't notice that they're giving a middle-of-the-road performance. Wrong! The audience will notice. They may not be able to say it in actor vocabulary ("Hey, that actor made a choice but didn't fully commit to it!"), but they will see someone waffling on-stage. Trust me. No one wants to see a waffling actor.

Rehearsals are for trying out choices. That's what you do. So if you're fortunate enough to play either Masha or Vershinin in *The Three Sisters*, and you're faced with that delicious scene in Act II, you spend the rehearsal period experimenting with choices. Are they having an affair? If so, how far has it gone? When did they start? Are they not yet having an affair? If so, how often are they alone? How did they get to be alone this evening? How long have they been alone? Were they outside like the rest of the family, or have they been walking around the house? Why are they coming into this particular room? What is the nature of their relationship?

Do they ever make physical contact? Has he ever told her he loves her before this scene? Why is she talking about the chimney? Is she avoiding talking about something that just happened? Is he really interested, or is he merely thinking of how he feels about her? When he says, "I'm thirsty. I'd love some tea," is he genuinely thirsty? Or is he trying to change the subject? Or is he trying to get her attention in some way? Or is this code for something else? (He never mentions the tea again, and, in fact, one page later he's declaring his love for her, which leads to a whole new set of questions: Has he ever expressed himself like this before? If so, what's different? If not, why tonight?)

The point is that there are a ton of choices to be made here, none of them right or wrong, but all worth exploring. And where do you do that exploration? In rehearsal.

The problem with many inexperienced actors is that they settle for the first choice they make. Even if a choice feels good the first time out, don't content yourself by settling with it. Try a second choice, and then a third. There will be plenty of time to go back to the original choice if that was truly the one that worked best. And you'll return to that choice with the full confidence that it is indeed the best possible option.

One of the most mesmerizing moments I have ever seen was Derek Jacobi as Cyrano de Bergerac on Broadway. At one point, sitting downstage left, he poured out a bit of wine on a table and slowly, languorously, *committedly,* dipped and draped the sleeve of his white peasant shirt into the blood-red liquid. Why did he do it? I don't have the faintest idea. Did it make sense? Not under normal circumstances, but here it did. Why? Because he was so committed to it that he pulled it off. He was so committed that he could have pulled off anything. This "nonsensical" gesture became one of the most arresting, poetic, poignant moments of that entire play. And of any play that I have ever seen.

The moral? Make a choice! And commit to it!!

Lesson 37:
Be Not Afraid of Silence

Sounds almost biblical, doesn't it?

Good. It should.

If, as we said before, each scene is a battle to be won; what are your weapons? What do you have to work with? The words of the play, certainly. That's your main source of ammunition. But be careful not to make the mistake that many actors make and let it be your *only* source of ammunition. There are other weapons too, and one of the strongest of those is silence.

Who says we need to talk all the time? Sometimes we make our biggest statements in life by not talking, not answering, not replying. Sometimes, too, the most emotional moments hit us when we're listening, when we're trying to speak but unable to formulate words.

Think back to the first date scenario. If all has gone well and the two have achieved their objectives ("Yes, I like this other person, and this other person likes me"), then perhaps the opportunity will arise for the all-important First Kiss. And isn't there usually a wonderfully awkward silence before that first kiss? It's not usually talk that leads into that first brushing of lips; rather, it's that sudden locking of eyes and the realization that you each want the same thing and that slow lean-in and slight angling of faces and — *presto!* — the first kiss happens. Isn't that how they often occur? With *silence* preceding that event?

If, on the other hand, a couple has an argument, isn't there oftentimes silence that accompanies that event as well? It's a heavy, anticipating silence, where each person is stewing and planning their attack, and when the first words of the argument begin, the floodgates open and the argument ensues. Then, within that argument, there are further moments of silence, where each combatant re-groups and thinks about her next plan of attack.

When you're told an emotional bit of news, isn't there silence that accompanies that moment? Maybe you want to respond verbally, but the emotion is too strong and won't let you. That's silence, too.

My point is that we don't use silence nearly enough in our acting, and when we do, it's a pre-planned silence *that isn't filled.* Silence does no good if it's silence for silence's sake. It must be filled; it must be genuine. As acting teacher Sanford Meisner said, "In the theater silence is an absence of words, but never an absence of meaning."

I would like to see actors make the choice more often to employ silence in their scenes. They have no problem finding silences when they do serious improvisations. The problem arises when they see the words on the page and just assume "this line follows that line, which follows that other line," and they don't allow silence anywhere in the scene.

Allow silence. Remember, most contemporary playwrights won't put in every place where they think a pause could go, and besides, it's far more interesting if the actors discover those moments for themselves, rather than merely following the directions of the playwright.

Pay attention to your daily life. Notice where silences occur. Then put them in your acting. You'll find they're as valuable — if not *more* valuable — than the words themselves.

Don't be afraid of silence. After all, it's golden, right?

Lesson 38:
Less Is More

It's a cliché, yes, and I hesitate to even mention it because of that fact, but it's true. Less is more. It's that simple.

Actors love to get in the way of themselves. They love to add layer after unnecessary layer to their acting, all in the name of creating the definitive character.

But you know what? Less is more.

Look at people. It's the less we do in our real lives that says so much about us. The subtle gesture. The sly glance. The easy manner of speaking. And while some people are more "out there" than others, it's the little things in their behavior that say the most about them.

But what is often our first temptation as actors? To show. To indicate. To make it big. To work too hard. Remember: Actors work way too hard on-stage because they don't work nearly hard enough at home. If you're thinking about your character *away from rehearsal,* you'll give yourself an honest chance to make true and subtle discoveries *at rehearsals.* This will allow you to trust your true and simple choices. And remember, it's not a case of working harder; it is a case of working *smarter.*

So try going the other way with it. Try doing less. Believe me, it will be more.

Lesson 39:
What Just Happened?

We don't live in a vacuum.

Things happen to us, and those things affect what we do and how we do it. They can be small things, they can be big things, but we carry those events with us. If you want to ground your acting onto something real (and that is, after all, the purpose of this book), then before every scene, before every entrance, ask yourself, "What just happened?" What events just took place that will affect your behavior in the scene?

We do a disservice to our acting if we don't figure out what just happened the moment before.

I see it all the time in classrooms. I will intentionally arrive early, before the first students, and watch them file in. Each student brings in a different energy, a different attitude, a different expectation, based largely on *what just happened*. A girl will come in smiling. Why? Maybe because she was just complimented in the hallway. Another girl comes in sullen. Why? Maybe because she broke up with her boyfriend last week and she just saw him flirting shamelessly with someone else (maybe the first girl). A guy comes in laughing. Why? Maybe because he just ran into his best buddy, who told him a funny story. A girl comes in with puffy eyes. Why? Maybe because she just found out a grandparent is sick and near death. Another guy comes in panting, wildly throwing his backpack to the ground. Why? Maybe because he couldn't find a parking place and he thought he was going to be late. Another boy comes in smirking. Why? Maybe because he just flirted shamelessly with a girl in class, but he can't be too brazen about it because his ex-girlfriend is in the class as well (you know how incestuous acting classes can be).

Preceding events affect the following events. What we do now is influenced by what we just did, by what just happened.

Actors, then, need to do this very simple homework and figure out what just happened to their characters. Then they can bring this energy with them on-stage. Again, the intention isn't to *show* the audience what just happened; it's merely to create a fuller life for the character, which will make your acting all the more believable. It's usually not important that the audience be able to understand exactly what just happened to you; they just need to know that you're entering the stage as a believable human being, and human beings carry their pasts with them.

When do you do this homework? Rehearsal, of course. Play with it. Make a different choice each entrance and see how it affects you. See what it does for the on-stage life of your character when you supply some history. If it's inappropriate for the character, or if it distracts from what the scene is about, the director will be sure to tell you. But believe me, directors are thrilled when actors take the initiative and make these choices on their own. It makes their job all the easier.

Some people refer to this aspect of acting as "the moment before," which is a perfectly good phrase. The two are synonymous. Knowing the moment before is knowing what just happened. And remember, as with all these lessons, it's not enough to keep the answers in your head. These aren't intellectual exercises. The trick is to incorporate your findings into your playing of the character, and let it begin before you ever step on-stage. Why? Because it all happens in that moment before; it all starts off-stage.

Asking yourself that simple question — "What just happened?" — and then bringing that new knowledge on-stage with you adds a fullness to your character that will easily take your acting up a notch.

Lesson 40:
Step Forward, Not Back

Believe it or not, I'm not speaking metaphorically here, I'm speaking literally. Don't let yourself step backwards on-stage.

Here's why. Most characters in plays are active. That's why we respond to them; they're going after something and they're active in their pursuit of it. When people in real life are actively pursuing something, they will step forward or they will plant themselves or they will occasionally pace, but they will never step backwards. Not metaphorically, and certainly not physically. Active characters don't step backwards, at least in their moments of greatest pursuit. It's only the weakest of weak characters who step backwards.

And yet I can't tell you the number of times I see inexperienced actors, in their big monologue, actually take a step or two backwards, away from the person (imaginary or not) from whom they're trying to achieve their objective. This is crazy! Active people move forward. Active people are unafraid to plant themselves. Active people do not step back.

Clear?

Lesson 41:
Avoid Attitude (Part One)

This is one of those lessons that work on more than one level. On the one hand, it's a fundamental lesson about acting. It might be tempting to play "in love" or "dangerous" or "pompous" (as the stage directions might say), and directors will often give you these very words as guidance, but playing attitude can't be done. Nor should it be attempted.

The best way to achieve an attitude is to understand the circumstances and objectives and then play the actions accordingly. The attitude will take care of itself.

So let's say the director (or the stage direction) says your character is pompous. All right. How do you go about achieving that? Not by playing attitude, but rather by figuring out your character's past. Why do they come off as pompous? And is that perhaps a defense mechanism for their own insecurity? If that's the case, their objective can be "to impress" — very playable and *very* active — and their action to achieve that objective can be to talk about themselves at length, to look down on others, to make their own work more important than others. In their heart of hearts they may not really believe these things, but they're trying to impress (that's what they want), and in that effort they come off as pompous. In that way, you, the actor have achieved the desired result without having to play the result. Make sense?

It seems simple enough, but it gets confusing when a director will tell you, mid-rehearsal process, "I need you to be more threatening." What do you do? If you're like most actors, your first instinct will be to *show* (that darn word again) the audience that you're threatening. You'll play an attitude. But this will only create a false sense of character. What you need to do, instead, is make a translation in your head. If your director gives you a character adjustment in attitude, you need to decipher that in terms of circumstances, wants, and actions. "Okay, the director wants me to be more threatening. Maybe I can raise the stakes of my objectives; I will kill this person unless they comply with my wishes. And what actions will I play? I will tease the victim, toy with them, and in that way I will come off as more threatening."

Again, the result has been achieved without playing for the result, because just as you can't play attitude, you can't play result.

You have to alter the causes that will appropriately affect the result. Not that the audience will understand this, nor maybe even the director. But if you want your character to be based in truth and believable on-stage, you need to make the adjustments through circumstances, objectives, and actions.

There's a simple acting exercise that demonstrates this pretty clearly. Ask for a half dozen volunteers to stand in front of the class. Then, give them various suggestions, such as "Be dignified," "Be dangerous," "Be cool." The rest of the class will no doubt get the giggles because there is nothing more comical and false than an actor trying to be a certain way, trying to play a certain attitude. Then, ask these same volunteers to count the number of chairs in the room. The difference is remarkable. All of a sudden, you have real actors engaged in a real activity (counting), and they are focused, they are intent, they are not self-conscious, they are even, in their own way, engaging. They're no longer playing an attitude; instead, they have an objective and they're playing an action. Big difference.

One of the most consistent traps I see actors (even good ones) fall into is "playing sexy." They know from the script that they're the love interest, or at least they're supposed to tempt the other love interest, and so what do many actors do? *They play attitude. They play at "being sexy."* And does it work? *No!! Never !!* (Sorry. I got carried away.)

I have seen very sexy actresses (sexy in real life) become completely un-sexy on-stage because they were playing at "being sexy." They not only didn't trust their innate sexuality, but they fell into the trap of playing an attitude as opposed to doing the work on the character's foundation. Why is this character sexy? Is it a result of their circumstances, their objectives, their actions? Do they know they're sexy? If so, they probably don't need to work very hard at being sexy; on the contrary, they can do very, very little, and that makes them all the sexier. And isn't that the way it is in real life? The sexiest people are those who appear to work the least.

One last point. There's nothing wrong about *achieving* an attitude. After all, it's only natural that an audience will say after seeing a production, "My, that one character was really sexy (or dangerous or charming or whatever)." The thing to remember is how to get there. You achieve attitude not by playing attitude, but by altering the circumstances, wants, and actions that help create the attitude.

As Uta Hagen wrote in her wonderful book, *Respect for Acting,*

"Settling for the 'mood' is as dangerous as going for an attitude. Spelled backwards, it is *doom* for the actor." (The italics are hers.) You cannot play mood or attitude. Instead, let them come about as by-products of the very specific work you're doing with circumstances, wants, and actions.

Lesson 42:
Find Stillness

One of the marks of the professional actor is the ability to find stillness on-stage, to allow yourself to be unselfconsciously still. It's not an easy task, especially at first, but my, oh my, what power you will hold once you nurture this skill.

The truth of the matter is that actors give too much away. Some over-gesture. Many sigh before lines. Many sigh *after* their lines. Many others move randomly about the stage. But the moments of greatest impact are often those of the greatest stillness.

So what's hard about being still? Well, try it. Have your friends tell you if you're capable of finding stillness when you do a monologue or a scene. If you're like most actors you probably shift from side to side or you have some nervous tic (tapping your toes, buckling your knees, fluttering your fingers). But the more comfortable you get on the stage — the more you believe in yourself and your character's intentions — the more stillness you can allow yourself. And then — *voila* — the more power you will have.

One word of warning. Your first attempts at stillness will probably fail. Because you will be so determined to find stillness that you will probably only manage to cut off each and every natural impulse you have.

Stillness isn't so difficult, but it takes practice. Like silence, it's a skill that requires belief in yourself (as both actor and character), as well as finding that balance between doing nothing and being simple. But, once found, stillness is a tool you will use over and over again because you will recognize the power you truly possess on-stage through its use.

Lesson 43:
Find Your Zone of Confidence

At some point in your acting life you've probably discovered that you're especially good at one aspect of acting. It might be comedy, it might be working with classical material, it might be movement theatre, it might be your ability to access emotion on-stage. Whatever it is, you know you're good at it.

Good! Build on that. Let that be your foundation. Allow yourself that confidence, and don't ever let anyone make you second-guess those talents.

I was amazed when I came out of graduate school and was suddenly getting beat out of certain roles that I knew I was perfect for — and the actors beating me didn't have any real "training" to speak of. Why was this? Because one of the down sides of graduate school for me was that I had learned so much in such a short span of time that I was suddenly questioning myself. It was as if I had too much knowledge, and so instead of having supreme confidence in my abilities, I found that I was second-guessing myself.

I've got news for you, as if you didn't already know: second-guessing comes through pretty loud and clear in an audition, and there's no director in the world who wants to work with an actor who is second-guessing himself. Directors want to work with actors who are confident in their abilities.

Gradually I came to understand that I did, indeed, have some talents and that all this self-questioning was not only unnecessary, it was harmful to my acting. Find those aspects of your acting with which you are confident (and let's hope there are many!) and play them to the hilt. Believe in yourself.

Now if, on the other hand, you don't have confidence in *any* of your acting abilities, well, maybe you should re-examine your desire to be an actor. Only *you* can give yourself the confidence you need to succeed in this profession. In other words, don't stand around waiting for someone to give you your life.

Find your confidence. Believe in yourself. Stand tall on-stage.

And if you don't have enough aspects of acting to believe in, then …

Lesson 44:
Work on What Needs Working On

None of us likes to be bad in anything, and all of us like to be good in something. There's nothing startling about that statement. In fact, that's probably why many of us went into theatre in the first place: it was something at which we were good. While our friends were finding success in other aspects of high school or college, we found we had an aptitude for being on-stage. Good.

Now, if we take the time to truly analyze our strengths and weaknesses within acting, we'll discover that we're good at some aspects and not as good at others. Natural enough. So what do we do? Our human inclination is to work on what we're already good at and neglect what needs the most attention. It's crazy, but it's true.

So I'm here to tell you to resist this temptation. In other words, don't be afraid to work on what needs working on.

So you're good with speech? Great. Now work on your physical awareness on-stage. So you're a natural with contemporary material? Terrific. Now focus on Shakespeare and Moliere. So you're a terrific singer? Excellent. Now concentrate on your dancing.

It is far too easy for us to focus only on those aspects at which we are already competent and ignore those aspects which need our utmost attention. I have known students in musical theatre programs who are tremendous tap dancers, but who are mediocre (at best) at modern and jazz. So what one single dance class do they sign up for semester after semester? Tap. Why? Because they're good at it. Fine, but don't neglect what needs working on.

You need to develop your skills as fully as possible so that when you begin to audition professionally you are the complete package. Work on your body, your voice, your speech, your singing, your skills with classical material, your improv, your dancing, your comedy, your tapping into emotion, your personalization, your playing of objectives, etc., etc., etc. Work on all of these elements and, whichever of these you are weakest at, *work on those the most*. Don't let yourself get stuck being a one-dimensional actor.

Being an actor is being self-employed, and it's up to you to evaluate the strengths and weaknesses of your business (which, if you didn't know, is you). If you have weaknesses as an actor, and it's only natural that you do, address them. Conquer them. Don't pretend no one will notice because — you know what? — they will.

Lesson 45:
Imagine

Show me an actor with imagination, and I'll show you an actor I want to cast. Here's a startling revelation that many actors may not want to face: you can have all the training in the world, but if you don't have a fertile imagination you'll never be a great actor. *Great actors have fertile imaginations,* and actors blessed with such imaginations make a playwright's (or a screenwriter's) words come to life in a way that the writers didn't even conceive.

You know those moments in the play or movie that stick with you long after the play or movie is over? Those moments we talk about later? That certain look. That certain gesture. That subtle way of brushing a hand against another's face. I can guarantee you those are moments borne of genuine creativity and fertile imagination. Not placed in there by the screenwriter or the director, but created by the actor who arrived at that choice herself.

This is why, as a director, I try to let my actors have as much creative reign as possible because I know that their choices will always be far superior to mine. Even if my choices are good, theirs will be better. Why? Because they're in the world of the play. But if they're the type of actor who is *waiting* for me to provide direction — telling them where to go and how to say their lines — the production will never rise above a certain level. It can't. It takes an actor's fertile imagination to do that.

In addition, there is the very practical element of auditions to consider. After seeing the same scene umpteen times, directors and casting directors are *thrilled* when an actor brings in his own original choices — when he honors the sense of the script and breathes his own original life into it. Directors want to work with such actors because they then know they can count on them to help carry the load of the film (or play or TV show); it won't all fall on the shoulders of the director. And directors like that.

Lastly, what do you do if you don't feel like you have a fertile imagination? Easy. Acquire one. That's why you see theatre and film and the best TV every chance you get. That's why you read voraciously. That's why you travel and see as much of the world and experience as many different cultures as possible. That's why you go to museums, galleries, symphonies, the ballet. That's why you hang out with people who will increase your own abilities and make you reach the top of your game. You do anything and everything to stretch your own imagination. And then, when that is done, you *allow* that imagination to come forth.

The great actress Laurette Taylor, famous for her portrayal of Amanda Wingfield, said that to work professionally, "personality is more important than beauty, but imagination is more important than both of them."

Amen.

Lesson 46:
Working at Home

I've already mentioned that actors work too hard at rehearsals because they don't work hard enough at home, and it should be clear by now that any time you're working on a role, you need to do much of the work on your own outside of the rehearsal space. (If you're working on a film, you could go so far as to say that you need to do nearly *all* of the work on your own, since film rarely provides the opportunity to rehearse.) So what's the most effective way to work at home?

This is an extremely individual decision, but, personally, I think the best time to work on your character — to think about your character — is to do so in moments where you're doing something else. While you're walking, for example. Or exercising. Or driving. Or doing the dishes. Gabriel Garcia Marquez, author of *One Hundred Years of Solitude* and winner of the Nobel Prize for Literature, installed an extra hot water heater in his house so he could take longer showers, because he recognized that's where he did some of his best thinking. Not sitting in front of the computer or the legal pad, but standing in the shower.

Personally, I feel the worst time to work on character is when you sit down on the couch and say, "Okay, now I'm going to spend the next hour figuring this person out." Maybe it's just me, but that's too logical a way to approach the matter, and my experience shows that actors who approach character in that manner end up with very "intelligent" choices, but choices that aren't necessarily terribly interesting. There are always actors out there who love to brag, "Oh man, I spent four hours last night working on my character." Remember: There's a difference between quality and quantity. It's very possible I can have a more fruitful experience with a thirty-minute walk than they can with their four-hour work session.

That's not to say that's a bad way to analyze text; on the contrary, when you're first trying to learn lines or scan Shakespeare, it takes that kind of deliberate approach. But when you're thinking about your character, I strongly believe you're far more liable to get in the wonderful creative side of your brain if you're engaged in some other activity. I've always found that my best ideas as an actor and writer come when I'm swimming or jogging or walking in the woods. I allow my mind to go blank, and all of sudden I am bombarded with original thought after original thought. I've cleared my mind of the clutter of daily life; I'm not forcing anything to happen, and all of a sudden wonderful thoughts come to me.

If you want to record those thoughts, I would encourage that as well. It's all too easy to come up with all these wonderful ideas, but then lose them half an hour later. Maybe write about your character in a journal dedicated to that play. Or maybe write a biography of your character. You would be surprised at the number of questions that will arise as you begin to do so. These writings aren't anything you need show anyone — in fact, I would encourage you to keep them intensely private — but they can be a record for you of your progress with the character.

Again, put yourself in a place where you are allowing the work to happen. Wherever that is, and whatever you're doing, keep searching for that place, that activity, that gets your creative juices flowing, where you feel safe to have idea after idea after idea. Allow the ideas to flow, and your character will be all the better for it.

Lesson 47:
Play Opposites

This is another one of those old clichés, right? You've done your homework, you've made some initial discoveries about the character, you're following your initial impulses, and then the director suggests, "Why don't you play the opposite of that?"

And you think to yourself, "Are they crazy?"

Not at all. There are a number of terrific reasons why you should look for the opposite. The first is what we talked about earlier: The whole point of the rehearsal process is to explore and experiment. If you go immediately with your first choices and never deviate, you'll probably present a rather straightforward and uninteresting portrait of your character. You'll be obvious. You won't surprise the audience at all.

If, however, you allow yourself the opportunity to explore other aspects of the character, including playing the very opposite of what you first suspected, you have a far better chance to create a character full of nuance — a character, in short, more closely aligned to real life. A character more likely to surprise an audience with his or her complexities. How much more interesting is that?

Another reason to find the opposite is that good writers have written it that way. A character may shout, "I hate you! I hate you!" but what's thrilling is when they mean "I love you! I love you!" Now that's interesting, and it's just the opposite of what the words would seem to imply.

One of the clichés often spouted by directors during the 1970s was, "Find the love." It seemed like after every scene a director or teacher would say, "Now where's the love in this scene?" It was so overused, it got to be something of a joke. But you know what? It wasn't a bad idea at all. Characters who carry some strong sense of distaste for each other will oftentimes have, at root, some kind of attraction. By "finding the love," you allow those complexities to come forth, as opposed to a two-dimensional portrayal of a character who is just mean or someone who merely yells. This latter seems to be the most common trap young actors fall into. While it may be fun to shout or yell onstage, it's necessary to find levels and justify such outbursts.

Hume Cronyn, regarded by many as one of the foremost character actors of the twentieth century, said he obeyed only one rule of acting: "If you're doing the devil, look for the angel in him. If you're doing the angel, look for the devil in him."

The perfect example of playing opposites.

Yes, follow impulses. See where they take you. But allow yourself to play opposites as well, and see where those choices take you, too. I bet you'll surprise yourself.

Lesson 48:
Take Your Time

If there's one mantra most new actors need to imprint on their brains it's this: Don't rush. Take your time.

Watch the great actors work. It all seems so effortless, so easy. And when we imitate them, we take the same time, luxuriate over the same pauses. We even kid ourselves that that's how we would have done the script if we had been given it first. Maybe. But for most people, that's generally not the case.

And the biggest difference has to do with taking your time.

Watching inexperienced actors at work in a play makes you think there's some big party happening after the show, at least based on the pace at which they rush through things. As a result, their mouths are working faster than their minds, so that they couldn't possibly have time to be thinking the things before they say them — unlike real life.

In life, we discover the images *before* and *as* we say the words, not *after*. The actor who is speeding along doesn't have a chance of being in the moment, because he's not allowing himself to find the images.

What's the rush? Take your time. Don't be afraid of silence. *Find the images*. Then you can speak.

Lesson 49:
It's Gotta Be the Shoes

This may seem nitpicky, but bear with me.

I'm not really a stickler for what actors should or should not wear in the classroom. Not really. As long as it doesn't bind them in any way, as long as they can be flexible (physically and emotionally), as long as they're willing and able to roll around on the floor and do whatever exercises are part of that day's agenda, I don't really care.

With one exception. Tennis shoes. This is the biggest impediment I see to the actor in the classroom.

Why? Very simple. Our feet inform us. We feel different if we're wearing dress shoes, as opposed to sandals, as opposed to high heels, as opposed to tennis shoes. As much as any piece of clothing or clothing accessory, our shoes inform how we move, how we walk, how we feel, even how we sit. With apologies to Nike, Reebok, and Converse, the actor who wears tennis shoes to class is an actor who's not allowing himself to stretch.

It's always been fashionable for young people to scuff their feet. My mom always said she never needed to sweep the hardwood floor of my bedroom because I always scuffed it clean. But I have news for you. There are very few plays — and even fewer characters — that call for scuffing on-stage. It's a rare play that has a teenager scuffing his or her way across the stage.

Tennis shoes lend themselves to scuffing, and as long as you wear them in class, you'll be tempted to fall back on old habits. Even though you may be working on Romeo, or Ophelia, or Henry V, or Lady Anne, your muscle memory will betray you if you're wearing tennis shoes, and all of a sudden you'll be an Elizabethan character with a scuffing problem. You'll move differently — and far more appropriately — if you wear any other shoe than tennis shoes.

When you're rehearsing a play, the first thing you should ask is what type of shoe you'll be wearing in the play, and from that moment on you should attend every rehearsal *wearing that type of shoe*, if not the very shoes themselves. You will be amazed at how shoes inform your character. And please don't be one of those actors (usually of the high school variety) who says, "I like to save all costume pieces for the final week, because then they complete me."

Yes, they complete you, but if you've been working with rehearsal costumes (especially shoes!) from the beginning, you'll find that sense of "completion" earlier in the rehearsal process, which will allow you to make even *more* discoveries before opening night. To the actor who says he likes to hold off on costume pieces, I say, "Why stop there? Why not hold off on learning your lines until opening night as well? That way, things will really be spontaneous on-stage."

(Sorry. I dripped a little sarcasm there.)

Because, in the grand scheme of things, you will be playing few characters wearing tennis shoes — and even if you do play a character with tennis shoes, you can get used to that feeling in a second — it's only to your benefit to wear *other* types of shoes to classes. Leave the tennis shoes at home. If you're serious about your craft, you'll invest in some other type of footwear that will be more beneficial to your acting.

There. Nitpicky enough?

Lesson 50:
The Power of Focus

I was doing a four-month run of an Equity waiver production in Los Angeles. The theatre held ninety-nine seats and was extremely intimate, and during the course of the play, in one of the most dramatic moments, the leading lady and I faced each other — she sitting on the chair, I sitting on the edge of the coffee table — and we expressed our true feelings for each other. We were holding hands, looking deep into each other's eyes, getting ready for the climax of the scene. At one performance — a matinee — at just that peak moment, an elderly lady leaned over to her companion and said, in a whisper loud enough to be heard by *everyone* in the theatre, "Look at the size of his Adam's apple." Ninety-eight people in the audience began to giggle, and it was a minor miracle that the actress and I made it through the rest of the scene without laughing ourselves.

The point is, if you're going to do this, you need to focus. You need to focus within the scene of a play (so that the loud stage whispers from the audience don't distract you), and you need to focus on what it is you want out of your career as well. You must focus on talking and listening while in the moments of the play, and you must focus on being a better businessperson to sell yourself as an actor. In short, you need focus in every arena of being an actor. Without it, you will be random and general (and uninteresting) on-stage, and have no clear direction in your career.

So how do you achieve focus? You allow it, of course. Too often actors will work too hard at focusing, as if it's something that can be achieved through a great deal of straining, like opening a jar. Far from it. True focus is simplicity in itself. It's concentrating on the tiniest of details. It's allowing yourself to listen, allowing yourself to respond.

The trap, then, with focusing is *over-focusing*. You see this all the time with inexperienced actors as they constantly stare at their scene partner on-stage, as if that were an indication of proper focusing. Or, in a monolog situation, they continually gaze straight ahead at that imaginary off-stage person. This is an improper form of focus because, by and large, real people in real situations (especially heightened ones) don't stare at other people. They don't constantly gawk at the person they're talking to. They look away. They find their thoughts. They look back to the other person and check in to make sure they're getting what they want them to be getting, *but they don't stare.* Besides, if you're looking non-stop at your scene partners on-stage, you're not creating any obstacles for them. Look away. Make them *earn* your attention. It's not only more believable, but it puts a better demand on your acting partners.

In terms of your growth as an actor, focus is listening to yourself as you determine where you want to go and what you want to do, and then following those impulses. It's setting a path for yourself and then following that path, not letting yourself get distracted by the myriad temptations and obstacles along the way. Maybe it's a simple word you place above your desk in your apartment (like "Persevere"). Maybe it's a picture of an actor you admire that you stick to the refrigerator with a magnet. Whatever gets you to focus on what you want is what matters.

Pablo Casals, the great cellist of the twentieth century, was quoted as saying, "Never let any external circumstances alter your purpose or disturb the calmness with which you pursue it." It's a beautiful statement, and one that applies both on-stage and off. On-stage, it fits perfectly with the importance of going after an objective and the need to follow through on that objective. Off-stage, it's just as applicable, stressing as it does the need not to be put off by the *many* obstacles that will come your way.

It's also a wonderful statement because the second part of it — "the *calmness* with which you pursue it" — implies that you go about your work with a steadiness of heart and mind. And it's true if you think about it. We're most successful in achieving our endeavors when we go about them simply, easily, calmly. Wonderful.

Focus, and great things can happen.

Lesson 51:
Don't Get Lost in the Mirrors

Not all that many years ago, I was directing a production, and our rehearsal space was a large makeup room surrounded by fifty mirrors. This was not a problem for most of the cast; we just got used to the fact that our reflections were everywhere, and we learned to ignore them. However, there was one actress ...

She was supposed to wear glasses in the role, and because she didn't wear glasses in real life, she spent a good deal of the rehearsal time looking at herself in the mirror, to come to terms with her new look. Fair enough. But her obsession with her mirror counterpart grew to dangerous proportions when she continued to look at herself during her scenes (when she should have been looking at her fellow actors) and during notes (when she should have been looking at me). It was obvious the mirrors were a major distraction to her, and I finally had to come out and tell her not to get lost in the mirrors. She did, and to her credit, she turned in a decent final performance.

I'm not suggesting you avoid mirrors. Far from it. Anytime you play a character and you have different makeup or hair (or glasses!), I think it's imperative that you study your face in the mirror so you know what you now look like. After all, you're familiar with how you personally look on a daily basis, and your character would likewise know how she looks on a daily basis, so it's to your advantage to study your "new face." It's just that there's a time and a place to do that, and rehearsal isn't that time. If you rehearse in a space with mirrors, and this is extremely common, don't let yourself get lost in the mirrors.

One of the negative results of getting lost in the mirror is that you get outside of yourself. You get outside of your body. You're looking at yourself from the outside in, and, suddenly, instead of being in the moment as the character, you're the actor examining and questioning each move you make. Instead of inhabiting the character's shoes, you're stuck in the actor's shoes and moving the character's shoes accordingly. This is no way to effectively play a character, and it's certainly no way to find truth on-stage.

If you want to believe in yourself on-stage, don't let yourself look in the mirrors when you're in a scene. Don't get lost in your own personal reflection, but rather on the people surrounding you.

That's where you should put your focus.

There's one other aspect about this worth mentioning. Inexperienced actors are often fond of doing line readings to mirrors to see how they look when they talk. Although this is a very individual thing, I would strongly recommend against it, for exactly the same reasons mentioned above. The more you get used to seeing yourself "while acting," the more self-conscious and out of the character you'll be. Your goal is to find truth, and when you do, you need to trust that truth to take care of itself on-stage.

If you're trying to manipulate your reactions based on your reflection, the best you'll do is create something that bears a resemblance to the truth. In other words, a copy of a copy of a copy. Not nearly so exciting.

There's a time for mirror work, it's true, but use it wisely and sparingly. While on-stage, the only eyes you should be looking into are those of your scene partner.

Lesson 52:
Build a Fourth Wall

In the theatre, the fourth wall is that imaginary wall that separates the actor from the audience. It got its name from the interior sets of the past which were designed with three walls on-stage — a stage right wall, an upstage wall, and a stage left wall — and the "fourth wall" was an imaginary one left open for the audience to view the events before them. Viewing a theatrical event was akin to an audience sliding the wall out of a doll house and peeking in to watch the goings-on before them.

So what do you do with this information?

Even though sets are, for the most part, radically different today, the concept of the fourth wall is still an important one, because it's the fourth wall that lets you share yourself with an audience. After all, theatre is based on the convention that you'll face forward, you'll speak up, your actions will be large enough that they can be seen and appreciated by those in the theatre, including the people in the very last row. And what the fourth wall does is let you find a way to *motivate* such sharing. For example, if you're doing a play in an interior set, you can place imaginary pictures, a window, or a mirror on this imaginary wall. If the scene takes place outside, then your fourth wall can be the vista before you, be it Agincourt in *Henry V* or the river in Act II of Chekhov's *The Cherry Orchard* or the barren landscape in *Waiting for Godot*. To invest in a fourth wall — to create a reality beyond the dimensions of the stage — is to devise a reason whereby you can face forward and not feel self-conscious about looking out.

One thing to bear in mind about the fourth wall is this: unless it's written in the script or the director gives you specific instructions, it's usually not necessary to make sure the audience understands every part of the fourth wall. In other words, you don't want to make the play suddenly about "admiring a painting on the fourth wall." The purpose of the fourth wall is to help you open up, but if it becomes a point of primary focus, chances are it will detract from the play. And even if it is important that the audience get some sense of what lies beyond the fourth wall, what's necessary for actors to remember (as always) is that they shouldn't feel obligated to show. Rather, by making those views real for themselves, they will become real enough for the audience.

Remember: Ninety-nine times out of one hundred, the fourth wall should be a means to an end, not the end itself.

Lesson 53:
Create Chemistry Correctly

Of the many aspects of acting that inexperienced actors needlessly worry about, creating chemistry has got to be near the top of the list. Finding themselves cast as romantic leads in a play, actors and actresses will often want to create that perfect chemistry so their scenes are believable. This usually leads to one of the two asking the other out for drinks after rehearsal, "so they can get to know each other better." Oftentimes, by the end of the evening, they do, indeed, know each other *much* better, to the point where they're dating and breaking up and then dating again all within the span of a single rehearsal period. I'm here to tell you this is death to a production.

By contrast, what the best actors have learned is that chemistry is really just a matter of truthfully pursuing wants. While I agree chemistry is one of the more intangible aspects of acting, it is best achieved when one character is trying to get something from another character, who in turn is trying to get something else from the first character. This is how chemistry is achieved. And if the script is clear and subtle enough to let the audience know these two are attracted to each other (or they're a happily married couple or whatever the circumstances), then the words do much of the work for you. All you need to play is the want. What do you want from the other character? What do you think they want from you? If you're playing a strong enough objective, the chemistry will be there.

Chemistry comes as the result of a truthful pursuit of an objective, pure and simple. Anything that requires more work than that will be false and unbelievable.

Lesson 54:
Fill the Pause

If ever there was a misunderstood playwright it would be Harold Pinter. Why? Because he has written all these "pauses" in his script, and actors don't know what to do with them. They pause, but they don't know why, so the pause becomes empty, tedious, filled with no meaning. Or they do know why, but they stretch the pause to ridiculous lengths, as if to make sure the audience "gets it."

Here's how to interpret a pause.

Stage directions are points on a map, steering you in the direction the playwright intended. Okay? Are you with me so far? A "pause" is one bit of direction used very frequently, but it's important to remember that these are not pauses for the sake of pauses. Rather, there is some *reason* for the pause, and it's up to the actor to figure out what that is.

Is the character suddenly moved? Has a new thought occurred to him or her? Is there that uncomfortable silence that punctuates so many of our conversations? Let the pause act as a *clue* that something is happening to your character, and it's your job to determine what that is.

Nor should you assume that there is one overriding meaning for the pause. Very likely there will be a different reason for each pause listed. It's up to you to get inside the script and discover those reasons.

Once discovered, you need to integrate that pause so fully into your performance that it ceases to be "pause" written on the page, but it becomes a sudden silence while a character, filling that silence, works through something.

Pauses need to be filled; they need to be active. And woe to the actor who suddenly stops speaking simply because the script tells her to.

Figure out why the pause was put there by the playwright, explore that reason in rehearsal, and let it happen of its own accord come performance. The pause will be filled, meaningful, and glorious, and might even carry more weight than the actual words.

Lesson 55:
What Do Line Readings Have to Do with Anything?

There's no winning with line readings. For some actors they are an insult. "I am an artiste, how dare a director stoop so low as to give me a line reading?" For other actors, they are everything. They crave the director who supplies them with an exact notion of how the line should be delivered.

Both groups are much deceived.

When you're in the moment, when you're truly talking and listening, when you're *truthfully* pursuing objectives, when you're personalizing, when you're using your imagination, *when you're doing all these things*, the line readings will take care of themselves. They will be there and they will be brilliant. Sure, once you're comfortable with your character, you can play with things a bit (playing opposites, toying with certain words or phrases, using pauses to your advantage), but if you're doing all the right things, the line readings should take care of themselves.

So from that point of view, I understand the actor who gets frustrated with the director who supplies him with line reading after line reading. That's a terrible way to direct, and such directors should be banished from the theatre. On the other hand, there are those occasions where the director — who is able to sit outside the action and hear things with a fresh ear — notices that if a certain line reading were altered it would produce a desired effect. From that point of view, I have no difficulty whatsoever with a director supplying an occasional line reading. Nor am I alone on this point. In *Method or Madness?*, the famed director and acting teacher, Bobby Lewis, vents his frustrations with actors who refuse to listen to line readings, claiming such direction will make them "phony." In this case, the director has the advantage of hearing the play from a neutral position, something the actor should take advantage of, not fight.

But my even bigger qualm is with the actor who relies on the director to supply the line reading, because that actor, whether they know it or not, is reducing the art of acting for *all actors*. By implying this is how actors prefer to work, directors will then feel comfortable providing more and more line readings, and again, if the actor is working properly, line reading notes should be kept to a minimum. While it's true that directors give actors line readings, we shouldn't mistake that for good acting. For the most part, directors give actors line readings because the actors aren't truly talking and listening.

Acting isn't about line readings. Acting is about achieving truthful behavior as a character on-stage and creating circumstances for yourself so genuine that things can happen for a first time. That's what acting is. Line readings come as a *result* of that effort. They're not the cause.

So what do line readings have to do with the overall state of acting? Very little. And actors would be better served by focusing on talking and listening (and wanting something and personalizing and using their imaginations) because those elements will lead to good and true line readings. Let the line readings come as a result. Don't try to manipulate them on your own.

Lesson 56:
Eliminate Clunkers

Ah, the clunker. Nearly every production has them. Just when the audience is willingly suspending their disbelief and entering the world of the play, just when they're experiencing empathy with the characters and about to have a cathartic experience, along comes a clunker and, *thwack*, the audience is once more outside looking in. No longer sharing that empathetic reaction to the character, they are now merely passive spectators.

What's a clunker, you ask? A clunker is any line (or gesture or piece of blocking) that you don't own. It's something you say or do on-stage which is all too obviously coming from the actor and not the character.

For example, you may be doing a beautiful job with a role. The audience is involved. You and your scene partners are engaged. Things are going well. And all of a sudden you have a line that you never really came to terms with. A line that has always sounded a little false. Or maybe it's a piece of blocking the director gave you at the last minute and you haven't quite motivated it, so it looks like a piece of blocking the director gave you at the last minute. Or maybe it's the way you handle your brandy snifter if you don't have experience with brandy snifters. Whatever it actually is, a clunker is the line or action that sticks out like a sore thumb and takes the audience out of the play. You may be able to get the audience back in the play, but oh, the production would be far improved if you never lost them at all.

Michael Weller is an American playwright who had a string of hits in the 1970s. Because he wrote of relationships — and was able to accurately portray the ups and downs of dating and marriage — his plays are beautifully written and still relevant today. But sprinkled throughout his plays are certain words that were popular in the '70s, but not so today. "Babe" is one of them. His couples often refer to each other as "babe." Now this isn't the most startling thing in the world, and goodness knows there are still people today who refer to their significant other as "babe," but the word isn't nearly as popular today as it was then. So what happens is that an actor will be playing the scene, and playing it well, and all of a sudden that "b" word raises its ugly head. The actor says it, and it sounds completely false. Whereas a moment before I had been invested in the scene as an audience member, now I'm out of it, watching it with a detached curiosity, thinking to myself, "Wow, weren't the '70s a weird time?"

Why? Because the actor didn't own the word. The actor didn't come to terms with that usage. The actor didn't eliminate the clunker.

So how do you get comfortable with that word? Simple: Practice. The more you rehearse the scene, the more comfortable you'll be with all the language. And if there are certain words — or actions or pieces of blocking — that seem especially unnatural, then I suggest you spend extra time with those moments. If it's the word "babe" that's throwing you, begin to say it outside of rehearsals. I'm not suggesting you suddenly refer to your local grocery clerk as "babe" (although that would get an interesting reaction), but allow yourself the opportunity to say the word outside of the theatre, even if it's on your own. In that way you'll begin to create some true ownership.

If it's holding a brandy snifter, do some research. Find out how people hold brandy snifters, and then practice at home. I can guarantee you there won't be time at rehearsals for the director to call a special brandy snifter holding session. It's something you need to do on your own. So find out how people do it, and if you don't own one yourself, buy a brandy snifter for your own personal use. Drink orange juice out of it, or milk. No matter. Just get in the habit of holding it. That way it'll become second nature, and you will have effectively eliminated the clunker.

One last thing about clunkers. I am convinced that the vast majority of the time, we're semi-aware of the clunkers we have in a production, but we hate to admit them. We desperately hope we can sneak them by. Be honest with yourself. If there's something that you feel is a potential clunker, *address it*. Deal with it early on. I guarantee that if you have any insecurity with it, it'll show on-stage. It'll be a clunker moment, and the audience will drop out.

Don't let them. Eliminate the clunkers, and the audience stays with you. It's that simple.

Lesson 57:
Do the Thing

Sometimes in rehearsal you'll be tempted to fake something, to mime a prop that isn't there, to pretend to drink water that doesn't really exist in the prop glass you're holding, to go through the motions of folding laundry without having any laundry to fold.

Avoid this.

Nothing can take you out of the moment quicker than having to mime. It doesn't matter that you don't have the actual prop you'll be using in performance, the key is to use *something*. It doesn't matter that the play calls for beer and you'll actually be drinking tea, make sure there's tea (or water or *something*) in that bottle when it comes time for rehearsal. Why? Because you need to actually *do* on-stage. You need to go through the real, sensory aspects of these activities, and if, in the middle of the scene, you drink from an empty glass and have to pretend to be swallowing, then all of a sudden you are doing a pantomime and not the play you had been doing a moment before.

In *Sanford Meisner on Acting*, Meisner is quoted as saying, "The foundation of acting is the reality of doing." And yet too many actors are all too content to let themselves drop out of the moment to mime (or indicate) an activity or motion instead of actually doing it. Don't let yourself.

Actually do the thing. Find some substitute prop so there can be that tactile feel of object in hand as you perform whatever activity it is you're called on to perform. Don't fall into the trap of miming; actually do. Your acting will be the better for it.

Lesson 58:
Leave the Work at Home

The work on a character happens at home, it happens in the rehearsal room, it does not happen in front of an audience. When you step on that stage it's important that you know objectives, actions, and circumstances so well that you don't need to remind yourself of them, you don't need to think of them at all. Once you step on that stage in front of an audience, you need to live entirely, exclusively *in the moment,* and if you're still conjuring up images of a dead pet from the 7th grade, or reminding yourself of the minutiae of your character biography, you won't stand a chance of being in the moment.

At his first NBA All-Star Game, 19-year-old Kobe Bryant displayed some awe-inspiring moves that literally took people's breath away. The moves were dazzling, rivaling the kind of wizardry we expected only from Michael Jordan. Asked afterwards if he'd been practicing on those particular moves, Bryant answered, "No, I've used them on the playground, but when I step on the court I rely on instincts."

A better acting lesson was never given.

Lesson 59:
Allow Yourself

You might have noticed one particular word that keeps popping up in these lessons: allow. It's as important as any word in the actor's vocabulary. All too often, actors get in the nasty habit of working too hard on-stage; they want to force their emotion, or demonstrate their objective, or make sure the audience understands certain physical conditions of the scene. Not only is such forcing unnecessary, but it works against the truthfulness of acting in general.

A better approach, and a simpler one, is to allow.

Here in America, especially, we always want to *force* things. We want to muscle our way through life, which is a terrible trap for the craft of acting because it leads to showing. By forcing (and pushing, and shoving, and *making things happen no matter the cost*) we don't allow the natural impulses to come forward. In fact, we even create a barrier between ourselves and our impulses, so that we can never truly be in the moment.

Once you've done all the work — you've worked on your body, you're comfortable with following impulses on-stage, you've done all your homework with regard to circumstances and wants and actions, you've thought about the character and made a number of choices, you've personalized her life, you've particularized the details, you're at ease on-stage with talking and listening — once you've done all this work, then you can truly *allow* the work to happen. You don't have to force it. On the contrary, there is nothing so disheartening as seeing an actor "at work."

As I've said before, I am a firm believer that actors don't work hard enough at home, and they work far too hard at rehearsal. (Another way of putting this is that actors try too hard in rehearsal because they haven't worked hard enough at home.) If you truly do the necessary work, both in terms of you as an actor and also as the character, rehearsals are a time to experiment. They're a time to allow all that good work to come forward. The problem, quite honestly, is that all too many actors don't start thinking about the work until maybe a half hour before rehearsal, and so when they get to rehearsal, they're trying to *force* everything: Emotions, characterization choices, personalization. All of it. If you do the work at home — on yourself and on your character — then all you need do at rehearsal is *allow*.

The great acting teacher Charles Jehlinger once said: "Good actors make things happen. Great actors let things happen, and then join them." I'm not suggesting you be passive on-stage, but rather that you trust that you've done the work (assuming you've done it) and that the work will come forth in an appropriate manner.

That's the spirit you want. *Allow* your own imagination to come forth. *Allow* the emotions to flow. *Allow* yourself to pursue objectives believably. Allow, allow, allow. It's far more interesting to watch an actor allowing than an actor forcing, and far more effective as well.

That said, and having taken all the class and rehearsal lessons to heart, it's time to turn to the performances themselves.

Andrew Nelson, Brandon Breault
Photo by Brett Groehler
University of Minnesota-Duluth

Performance

Lesson 60:
Honor Directors/Beware of Directors

The actor existed before the director. For nearly 2,400 years, in fact.

While it's true actors have always had someone "directing" the production — many times the playwright (e.g., Sophocles, Moliere), sometimes someone within the company — it wasn't until 1854 that George II, the Duke of Saxe-Meiningen, recognized the need for a unifying power and the value of some one person exercising an artistic vision. He then became, for all intents and purposes, the first director. (Remember this if you're currently enrolled in Theatre History.) Looked at that way, written theatre has existed for 2,500 years, but the role of "director" was born only 150 years ago.

And yet actors — not directors — have consistently been at the bottom of the food chain, partly because there are so many actors, and partly because they're willing to do whatever it takes to act, to be in a show and make that incredible contact with an audience night after night.

Remember how I said that anyone can act? Well, anyone can direct as well. Don't get me wrong, there are terrific directors out there who know how to put together a successful theatre production and who understand how to deal with actors in the process. I myself am indebted to a number of highly skilled directors who got performances out of me that I never would have gotten from myself without their help. Never. Not in a million years. But there are also many directors out there who aren't so talented. That's okay. After all, chances are that when you start out as an actor you're rather rough yourself. But you need to remember not to give away your worth as an actor merely to please a director, especially if you have more to offer than that particular director.

For example, the most important word in theatre is "engagement." Actors need to engage other actors on-stage, and they need to engage an audience in the process. Some directors are more concerned with stage pictures, with concepts, with their own all-important vision, and in the process they neglect — either from lack of experience or lack of true theatre knowledge — what happens in the actor's soul.

But you must not forget what happens in the actor's soul. You must not forget to engage other actors on-stage. You must not forget to make a real, palpable connection to the audience. One of the directors I admire most these days is Daniel Sullivan, who, as of this writing, has won one Tony award and been nominated for four others. In a July 9, 2001 interview with the *New York Times*, he was quoted as saying, "I just find there is an energy that runs through a play that has to do with the connections between characters. And finding that nuance and finding a way for the actors to understand the power of it is the thing that obsesses me most." It's pretty clear he values the engagement between actors as his highest priority.

Now I have nothing against a director with a strong-minded approach to a play (whether he calls it a "concept" or a "vision" or his "dramatic action" is irrelevant); in fact, that's exciting. Nor do I have a problem with a director setting a play in another context (e.g., *Much Ado About Nothing* in post-World War I England or *Hamlet* in post-apocalyptic America). Personally, I think anything that makes theatre now, real, *alive*, is all for the best. But. I do have a problem with directors who make that the overriding concern and neglect the acting in the process.

Of course, what makes it tricky for the actor is that she must listen to what each director is telling her and translate that into her own acting vocabulary. And, as you no doubt know, each director works differently. When I was in college, playing my first major role in a play, there was one scene between the leading actress and myself that we couldn't get right. We devoted two hours one evening to this particular scene, while the director watched us in silence, giving us little concrete direction. All we knew was that the scene wasn't working and it was basically up to us to fix it. Finally, at the end of the two hours (and very little progress), the director ambled forward, cleared his throat, and said the following few words: "Thomas, I guess what I want from the scene is deep purple, not light blue." That was it. Deep purple, not light blue. That was the most specific direction he gave me all evening.

Again, each director works differently, and each actor responds differently. For some actors, that would be a perfect bit of direction. For someone like myself at the time — a sophomore trying to understand how all the pieces fit together — it was of little help, and my mind scrambled to translate his direction into something that I could apply to my acting.

Remember two things: (1) in the grand scheme of things, it was the actor who came first, and (2) it's the actors with whom the audience connects. Take away the actor and we'd be looking at a slide show. Given a choice between a director who insists on showing off how creative he or she is (so we're always aware when watching the play of the director's many contributions to "help" the play), or a director who makes it all look effortless, who makes it appear as though the play and the actors were brilliant enough that it could have directed itself, I'll take the latter any day.

So how can you tell the good directors from the bad directors?

The best directors elevate, inspire, cajole, shape, create, and allow you to create. The worst directors tell, demand, show, insist, relegate, and give you no freedom in the creative act.

And the frustrating part of it is that we, as actors, allow it to happen. Time and time again. We're so desperate to work, and — worse — so desperate to *please* that we'll do whatever the director asks of us, believing it's all for the greater good. In short, we're just too trusting.

I expect a lot from actors. Let's face it, making a living from acting is the greatest gift in the world. What a rush! What a great job. But, as always, with privilege comes responsibility. Actors need to stay active, they need to stay in shape, they need to be well-read, they need to continue to see great theatre and film, they need to continue to create each and every time they perform, not letting themselves fall back on old tricks in the process.

The director has responsibilities as well, and the greatest of those is to allow the actor the freedom to create. If you run across a director who doesn't give you that freedom, run — do not walk — *run* as fast as you can. Because you know what? That is not a real director.

Don't try to please.

Don't accept directors who merely tell you how to do it. Engage them in discussions, and if you disagree, make a case for yourself. Stand up for yourself. A good director will respect you for it.

Don't accept directors (or teachers, for that matter) who insist on name-dropping to prove their worth — make them deal with *you*. Make them give you concrete advice.

Directors can bring so much to the theatre, but don't be fooled into thinking that they are the be-all and end-all. It is the actor who connects to the audience. It is the actor from whom the audience experiences the play. It is the actor who provides the passion, not the director.

Again, the best directors can help you get there in ways you can't even imagine. The worst directors handcuff you into doing a pale imitation of the blocking they have given you, allowing no chance for you to be an artist in the process. Be discerning actors. Be able to tell the good directors from the bad directors, and respond accordingly.

Lesson 61:
Don't Save It for Opening Night

Every once in a while, you will run into an actor who gives one kind of performance in rehearsal and another kind in performance itself. If you ask this actor why they appear to be marking it in rehearsal, they'll often respond, "I don't like to use everything up in rehearsal. I'm saving it for opening night."

Let me tell you right here and now how dangerous — and stupid — such a notion is.

Rehearsals are about experimenting. They're about testing what works for your character and what doesn't. They're the best time to truly go for it, to push those limits of yourself to see what you can get away with for that particular role. If you ever hold back, emotionally or otherwise, you're not giving yourself a chance to truly explore what you need to explore. And if you do go for it — really go for it — night after night in rehearsal, think how far you will have stretched and how much further you'll then be able to go in performance, without your being aware of it. Whether they realize it or not, the actors who hold back and "save it for opening night" are admitting their lack of confidence and skill in their abilities. The true actor has no need to hold back in rehearsal, because the true actor will be able to create circumstances so alive that each time they step on-stage — be it in rehearsal or performance — truthful behavior will emerge, no matter how heightened that behavior might be.

There's another aspect to holding back as well, one that is more damaging to the play as a whole, and that is what happens to your fellow actors. If you hold back during rehearsals and "save it" for opening night, your fellow actors will not have a chance to know what you'll be doing come performance. Granted, this will make things very alive and spontaneous on-stage — for a performance or two — but it's equally likely that the play could then turn into a big muddy mess. The playwright and director have shaped the play in such a way that there is a logical and natural build to the order of events. If you're one of those actors who saves things for opening night, chances are you're one of those actors in love with intensity, no matter the cost.

Film is a different matter. In that medium, it's not unreasonable to do the same scene, shot from different angles and with varying setups, a hundred times over the course of a day. In that case, you do want to save something for your close-up, especially if it's an emotional scene for your character. While not exactly "marking" your acting, you do want to keep a little something in reserve for the all-important close-up.

But theatre is different.

In theatre, it is the actor's responsibility to serve the play, and you do so by presenting a believable character in keeping with the context of the play. The most effective way to discover that character is through rehearsal, not waiting for opening night.

Show me an actor who saves it for opening night, and I'll show you an actor I don't want to be on-stage with, especially during the course of a lengthy run.

Lesson 62:
Make Things Happen for a First Time

One of the better definitions of acting, voiced by the late, great acting teacher Sanford Meisner, is "Acting is making things happen for a first time." I love that definition because (1) it's so wonderfully true, and (2) we tend to forget it over and over again.

Every time you step on that stage, be it rehearsal or performance, things have to happen for a first time. You have to start over. You have to pretend you don't know the outcome of the play. You have to pretend you've never done this play before. You have to pretend you've never said — or heard — these words before. Why do actors forget this? Because they've been rehearsing the play for four (or five or six) weeks. Because they've been performing it for an audience for one week (or two weeks or ten weeks). Because they know the lines inside and out and have gotten into the bad habit of not listening, either to themselves or to their scene partners.

But to truly be in the moment, to truly be a successful actor, you have to hear things for a first time, and you have to say things for a first time. You have to make *discoveries* each and every time you say the words. You have to put yourself in a place where none of this has happened before. You have to allow yourself to be surprised each and every night, to be amazed, to be saddened, to be exalted.

Now that you know the lines, now that they are truly a part of you, you don't have to think about them. You can trust that they will be there for you. Another character says a line, and that prompts your line. You don't have to worry about it in advance (which would take you out of the moment); you can trust that your line (and gestures and blocking) will be there.

And once you know these lines and trust that they are there, you know what happens? Things happen as if for a first time. Remember, for these characters, this is the first time they're saying these words. This is the first time they're performing these actions. They don't know the end of the script — they don't know there's a script at all. This is all happening *in the now*. And your supreme goal as an actor is to make it look as though none of this has ever happened before. Your ultimate objective is to make it appear as if things are happening for a first time.

Don't assume that each speech you say is something you've

thought about for years. On the contrary, it's far more interesting (and *dramatic* and *theatrical*) if this is the first time you've spoken these words. Your character may have *thought* about these concepts, but it's the first time you've been able to articulate these particular thoughts.

Now this is tricky. After all, you've just spent the last month in rehearsals; by now you should be pretty familiar with the play. You know what you'll say; you know what your fellow actors will say. You know where to go and when to go there. But you must hide all this. You must *discover* these words, these gestures, this blocking. You must perform them because there's a *need* to perform them. You must make them happen for a first time.

One of the biggest downfalls I see in many college productions is that things aren't happening for a first time. The plays are, in many respects, slick. The actors go places and do things and say words, but for no apparent reason. It's clear they're carrying out the wishes of some supreme being (in this case, the director), but there's no apparent *motivation* for those actions.

You have to start in innocence. You can't let yourself *know* how the play will unfold; you must let it happen to you. You must forget last night's rehearsal where you cried in the final scene; you must pretend last week's standing ovation never happened; you must not anticipate that the character opposite you will turn you down when you ask him or her out. If you think of those things, you will be re-creating. You will be imitating yourself, as opposed to making things happen for a first time.

I have seen some amazing productions of plays go steadily downhill from opening night to the end of their run. They've gotten tighter and slicker perhaps, but less engaging in the process. They're cleaner, sharper, more expertly timed (all of which are good), but if they sacrifice the element of discovery, if things aren't happening for a very first time, the play will suffer. The audience won't be able to articulate it, and on a surface level they may even enjoy it. But on a deeper level, they will be missing something. And you, the actor, know what that is. It's the element of the human condition that makes live theatre so exciting. It's things happening for a first time.

Your job — and it's part of the reason why truly successful actors are able to command large salaries — is to make things happen for a very first time. You need to hear the words your fellow actors say as if you've never heard them before. You need to find reasons for every gesture and every bit of blocking. And you must discover the words you say, just as we discover the words when we say them in real life.

If any of this — words, gestures, blocking — comes out too easily, the audience will sense that something isn't right. Though they won't be able to articulate it, it will be clear that they're not watching genuine human behavior. And why not? Because in "real life," things happen for a first time.

Our stage lives should be no less immediate.

Start over. Each night. You owe it to your audience, as well as yourself.

Lesson 63:
Relax and Give Yourself a Chance

It's no secret that when the great acting teacher Constantine Stanislavski examined what made some actors more successful than others, and why some nights were more effective than others, he kept coming back to one thing: Relaxation. When actors are truly relaxed, devoid of unnecessary tension, they have a fighting chance of being successful on-stage, of being in the moment. But Stanislavski discovered that if they weren't relaxed, the likelihood of success was greatly reduced.

What do we mean by relaxation? Stretching out. Warming up. Learning to let go. Anything you do that rids yourself (your body, your voice, your mind) of unnecessary tension is a step in the right direction of relaxation, because tension, as Stella Adler declared in *The Technique of Acting*, "is one of the absolute enemies of acting."

You'll notice I keep using the phrase "unnecessary tension." The acting teacher Lee Strasberg is the one who coined it, who realized that some small amount of tension is desirable. After all, it's tension in the muscles that allows us to stand, to walk, to talk, to sit up straight. So we don't want to eliminate all tension and populate the stage with bunches of jellyfish, spineless beings who don't even have the muscle control to utter a sentence or walk from stage left to stage right.

We just want to eliminate unnecessary tension.

How do you do that? Warm up. Devise some fifteen-minute warm up that you can perform at the drop of a hat. Make sure the warm up includes a section on breathing, on the physical aspects of your body, and on your voice and speech. Determine an order that makes sense (starting with breathing is always good), and make sure you build progressively throughout the warm up. For example, you want to make sure the voice is warmed up before you start tackling tongue twisters and speech. I would also suggest you end on some "high note." Maybe finish off your warm up by working on some favorite, memorized bit of text. Or simply by "taking stage" — standing at the front of the stage or rehearsal room and taking in the space, giving yourself the authority and permission to enter into the world of the play.

When do you do these warm ups? Absolutely before every performance. Definitely before an audition. And I would even strongly suggest a warm up before rehearsals. After all, it's in rehearsals where the experimentation takes place, not in performance.

Will you be able to feel the difference? Without question. You'll be surprised at how much more range you'll have. It may be subtle, but it may be just enough to give you the confidence to try a new choice. It may be just enough that you suddenly don't feel awkward about where to put your hands. It may be just enough that you can try things vocally that you wouldn't have tried before. In other words, it will increase your range, it will add potential colors to your palette, it will open up new choices for you that will make your acting not only more grounded and believable, but also more varied.

Will warming up make you a good actor? No. But will it make you a better actor? Absolutely. Do all actors warm up? Not hardly. And there are some very good ones who don't do anything even resembling a warm up. I remember working with a pretty good character actor in summer stock whose idea of a warm up was to go to the loading dock, smoke a cigarette, and say "buddaga-buddaga" a couple of times. It got a big laugh from all of us, but you know what? Can you imagine how much better he would have been if he had allowed himself even ten minutes of warming up before a performance? Can you imagine how *every* actor would be so much better if they just allowed themselves that time?

Again, remember, you're not in competition with those other actors. You're only in competition with yourself, and you will definitely be better if you warm up.

Think about it. As a pianist, you wouldn't dream of taking the concert stage without some kind of finger exercises beforehand. As a singer, you would never let yourself step on-stage without practicing scales. As an athlete, you would never dare step directly onto the field (or onto the court or into the pool) without first stretching, loosening up, jogging, taking batting practice, shooting the ball, or whatever is appropriate for that particular sport.

So why do actors think they can get away with not warming up?

If you relax, you give yourself a chance to increase your range as an actor. If you don't, you could very well be stuck doing your same old schtick year after year after year. The choice is yours. Why not relax?

Lesson 64:
Simpler, Simpler, Simpler

The best advice I ever got from a director was this: "Simpler. Do it simpler." We were shooting a film, and he must have said it fifty times in a single day.

"Simpler, Tom. Do it simpler."

I have not forgotten it, and in many respects it was the single most important piece of acting advice I ever got.

While you might dismiss this mantra as being particular to film, I think it applies equally to stage. To put it another way, how little can you do to achieve what you want to achieve? Thought of in this manner, it will help you with the temptation of "showing." If you do less — if you keep it simple — it will be genuine behavior, it will prevent you from indicating, and the audience can more readily accept your character.

Yes, of course, there are those plays that require larger-than-life acting styles (farces, for example), but even there you want to make sure you're tied to something real and aren't going exclusively for result. Yes, you want your comic timing to be impeccable, but it's always more fun for an audience when you do less, because it often reads as more.

Another way to think of this is to compare it with a painter using brush strokes on a canvas. As an actor, how small a brush stroke can you make for your character to achieve what you (and the director and playwright) want you to achieve? For me as an audience member, the smaller the brush stroke, the more satisfying the result. When an actor consistently uses large brush strokes, I feel force-fed as an audience member, and that doesn't make for a satisfying evening of theatre.

The simpler your actions to achieve your goals, the more satisfying — and real — your character will be.

Simple enough?

Lesson 65:
Deny the Lie

With the exception of a couple of second graders I know, people are pretty good liars. They do enough of it in one form or another to be fairly skilled.

So why is it in so many plays characters come off as such bad liars? Why are we constantly hit over the head with the fact that a character is lying? Because the actors are making sure "the audience gets it."

You know what? The audience is smarter than you think, and it's always a mistake to talk down to an audience. They'll figure out if someone is lying or not. And if they don't get it, well, that makes it all the more interesting for them. "Is that character telling the truth or not?" they'll ask themselves. Good! That's engaging.

What's not good is the legion of actors who feel the need to show the audience they're not telling the truth, either by adding a catch to their voice, suspiciously looking away, or suddenly stumbling over the words. Granted, there is some element to most lying, *but does it need to be that obvious?*

As an actor, it's a far more interesting choice to deny the lie. Commit to your character's version of the truth. Truly hide it from the other characters (and the audience) that you're lying. Don't be so obvious. Don't feel the need to show.

If you deny the lie it will not only be more believable, but also far more interesting.

Lesson 66:
Don't Give Away the Mystery

Why is it that as normal, everyday, regular people we're so engaging, but put us on the stage and our first instinct is to deny all that's wonderful and interesting and subtle about us? I'll tell you in one word: Mystery.

Part of what makes us interesting in real life is the fact that there's an element of mystery to each of us. We have secrets. We can't be completely figured out; it's not possible to fully understand any person. In fact, isn't it just the opposite? Just when you think you know someone inside and out, they do something that completely surprises you. That's called human nature, and it's why we're a fascinating species. It's why books are written and movies made and plays performed. The human being is an interesting animal. He can't be completely understood.

But what happens on-stage is we feel the need to tell the audience everything about us. We want to make sure the audience *understands* everything we're doing. We go to great lengths to make sure we're behaving appropriately as our character so the audience will *get it*. The reason this is dangerous thinking for actors is that what makes us interesting in the first place is our unpredictability — the sense of mystery.

So what am I saying? Don't give it all away. Keep some secrets for your character. (Remember: The theatre is one place where secrets are not only allowable but desirable.) Create those inner wants and ambitions which may (or may not) get fulfilled in the course of the play. Give yourself a full life. Find inconsistencies. Embrace them; don't iron them out.

And please, please, please don't feel the need to show or tell or explain everything to the audience. Make them work a little. After all, it's how we normally experience life, trying to guess the motivations of our friends and enemies, and if we as an audience have to put some effort into figuring out your character, *that's a good thing*. It's only boring and uninteresting when everything is presented to us all at once and there is nothing left to engage us. As the great film director Billy Wilder used to say, "Let the audience add up two plus two. They'll love you forever."

I remember playing a supporting character in a play in Los Angeles, and although my character's function in the play was to act as a sounding board for the female protagonist, I decided to add some circumstances for him that weren't in the script. Namely, I decided he was still in love with this woman. So there she was, spilling her guts out to me about this new man in her life with whom she was in love, and there I was, patiently listening and advising, but deep down, it broke my heart because I still loved her. Was this clear to the audience? Many of them guessed it, yes, but even those who couldn't figure it out knew something was up, and were far more engaged with the play than they would have been otherwise.

Logan Pearsall Smith once wrote, "What I like in a good author is not what he says, but what he whispers." Secrets and mysteries are the actors' whispers. The more they stay whispers, the more interesting those actors become.

Lesson 67:
Embrace Failure

Of all the lessons, this is may be the toughest. No one likes to fail, especially in this country. We all want to win, and win all the time. Well, I've got news for you. Winning is fine, but truth be told, we learn a lot more from losing. So my wish for you as you're first starting out on this path to better acting is that you fail, and fail often. I'm serious about this.

Look, here's how it goes. If you get cast in a play at college, you immediately think you deserved it. You think you've finally arrived as an actor; your ship has come in. But what you don't take into account, of course, is that maybe you're one of the few guys in the whole department, and all the guys who could sing and dance were cast in the musical, which basically left you. No, you never think of that. Nor do you really examine the audition, at which you flubbed lines and stepped all over yourself. Nor does it occur to you that you're the only actor in the department of a certain type who could play this particular role. It doesn't matter to the director that your talent level is low; the fact is, you're the right type for the role.

So the point is, you've gotten cast, but you haven't learned anything from the experience. You won't work any harder on your next audition (even though you didn't do particularly well on this last one), and at the following set of auditions you will just assume that you *deserve* to be cast because, well, you were cast before, weren't you? You haven't failed, and so you haven't learned.

The same might go for doing the play itself. Your family will say nice things. Your director will say nice things. Your friends will say nice things. Even the reviewer from the local North Dakota newspaper might say nice things. And again you will think it's all due to your enormous talent as an actor.

You haven't failed, and so you haven't learned.

You see, what we learn from failure is the desire to improve. You give a bad audition, and so you vow never to be unprepared again. You come to opening night and realize you still don't know who the character is you're playing, and so you vow never to use rehearsals as a time to socialize again. You give a mediocre performance the night an important producer (or director or casting director) is in the audience, and you vow to never give an inadequate performance again.

As Seneca wrote over two thousand years ago, "Failure changes for the better, success for the worse."

The point is, when failure happens — when you give bad auditions, forget lines on-stage, don't get the roles you want, give less-than-stellar performances, get mediocre grades in acting classes where you should be doing better — that should serve as a wakeup call. You should take those signs seriously and put them to your advantage.

There are countless success stories out there of people in all fields who have failed. They were disappointed because they didn't make the basketball team, they weren't elected Homecoming Queen, they weren't chosen for the cheerleading squad, the person they liked didn't like them back. And you know what those people did? They increased their energies into improvement, some into those same fields, others into different fields altogether. They used "failure" as a tool of motivation. It made them work harder.

And in the long run, they learned far more from those failures than from any "successes," especially early ones.

Don't be afraid of failure, and when it happens — and it will — embrace it. Use it as a means to improve yourself so that you won't ever have to experience it again.

Lesson 68:
Raise the Stakes

You've no doubt heard it in an acting class but maybe never bothered to ask for a definition. What does it mean to "raise the stakes"?

Simply put, it means to make things more important, more urgent. Every play — every *good* play, at any rate — tells a story with an inherent conflict. Remember, if there were no conflict there would be no drama. Characters are at odds with one another, or with the forces surrounding them, or even with themselves (or maybe all of the above). Plays are about those heightened moments in life when the conflict is greatest. It's an extremely rare play that is merely slice-of-life.

And yet there is a great tendency for actors "to get comfortable," to prove they can be realistically natural on-stage. What this leads to is a diminishment of the circumstances. Suddenly the actor is more concerned about proving how good she is, how relaxed she can be on-stage, how "life-like" she appears, and what she loses is the very drama itself. Actors forget that in real life, in circumstances similar to the play, people have an *urgency* to achieve their objectives, and that the objectives matter. Great plays are often written with life-and-death consequences, and it's the actor's responsibility to ensure those consequences stay present throughout the course of the play.

When a director or teacher tells you to "raise the stakes," what they're saying is, "Don't lose the importance (or necessity or *urgency*) of what's happening." Don't take the circumstances for granted. Don't anticipate that things will work out for the good (or for the bad, depending on the play). If it's a well-written play, the stakes will be inherently high, and it's up to the actor to make sure they stay at that level. With the stakes raised, the urgency to achieve objectives will increase, and the entire level of engagement (both between actors and other actors and between actors and audience) will suddenly increase as well.

I had one acting teacher who always said that if a scene wasn't playing as well as it could, the actors should simply raise the stakes and that would take care of much of the problem. He said if he were allowed only one fix-it suggestion to actors, that would be it. Raise the stakes.

It's one of the simplest — and most valuable — lessons in the theatre.

Lesson 69:
Allow the Emotion, and Then Fight It

It's not coincidental that the lesson on personalization was well before this one. Inexperienced actors love to speak of emotion. Perhaps because they have had little experience (or success) achieving true feelings on-stage, emotion always seems the Holy Grail of a young actor's life. And when you say "emotion," most actors immediately think of one thing: crying. Tears.

This is the single biggest mistake actors can make, for two reasons.

One is that there are so many more emotions than just sadness that we experience on any given day. In fact, crying and tears are probably the least of what we experience in our daily lives. Granted, plays are centered around heightened moments in our lives (see previous lesson), but, even then, tears make up just a small portion of our stage time. And yet inexperienced actors are fascinated with just such emotions.

"Do we get to cry in this class?" "Are you going to teach us how to cry?" "I really want to cry. Will you make me?" "I've always wanted to cry on-stage. Am I going to learn how?"

Don't ask me why this is, but many actors seem to think it's a badge of honor to cry on cue.

The reality is that we experience so many other emotions on-stage, and those need to be as real as anything we experience in our daily lives. Joy. Wistfulness. Envy. Pride. Anger. Remorse. Love. These are all emotions actors are called upon to experience, but actors discount them because they're not the big one; they're not tears. They're not crying. Well, let me tell you something. Because these others (pride, joy, etc.) are the emotions you'll explore through the majority of the play, it's essential you understand how to experience them truthfully. These "other" emotions are the bread and butter of any role. Neglect them, and you'll come off as false and disconnected. *Allow* yourself to experience them, and you'll come off as a real human being, a character with whom people can identify.

(Frankly, I think that genuine laughter on-stage is far more difficult to create than tears. It's tough to trick ourselves into laughing; it's not so hard to trick ourselves into crying. And as an audience member, there is nothing that takes me out of the play faster than an actor who is "fake laughing.")

So how do you experience these emotions? First of all, you allow. You let it happen. You mustn't force emotions out of yourself like you're laying eggs; you must allow them to happen. Focus too much on *making an emotion happen* and I guarantee you that it won't. But create circumstances for yourself where the emotion *can* happen, where you allow it breath, and you have a fighting chance.

You *personalize*. You ask yourself what things mean to your character and you let yourself truly experience them. As I said earlier, you can do this through substitution, or you can do it by simply believing in the circumstances of the play. No matter. The point is, you create the illusion (whether real or not) of your character experiencing the emotion.

This is why I'm such a fan of personalization, because it implies a connection with all the emotions you experience on-stage, not just the really big ones. It implies that every single emotion, no matter how small, will be real and heartfelt and genuine, which is what needs to happen if you're to be believable as a character. The actor's task is to store away as many moments, feelings, and sensory details as possible, and then be able, at a moment's notice on-stage, to access them. That's what an actor does. That's why actors need to be in tune with their surroundings and themselves, and why they need to be able to personalize. To personalize is to access that wonderful storehouse of emotions that each of us carries around throughout our lives.

I mentioned earlier that there were two reasons why the forcing of tears is a bad idea, and I've only discussed one of them. Here's the other: in real life, ninety-nine times out of a hundred, when we're crying, we're usually trying not to. We're usually struggling to contain those tears. We don't want others to see us cry, and that usually makes us cry all the more.

And that is the very thing that's compelling on-stage: not an actor crying freely like some circus performer, but rather someone struggling *not* to cry, and yet the crying happens anyway. Think about it. These are the moments in theatre and film that move us the most — the times when the character is struggling to keep their composure, to fight back the tears, to not cry. That's moving for an audience. That brings a lump to our throats. Why? Because we recognize ourselves in similar situations.

A final story. When I was in my twenties and living in New York City, I attended a church on Fifth Avenue, and one Sunday our minister gave his last sermon. He was retiring after serving fifty years of being a preacher, twenty-five of those in that very church. He was a popular minister who was a master storyteller, especially when it came to delivering sermons. So on this particular Sunday, the sanctuary was packed as everyone came to see and hear his final words, and an interesting thing happened. He was uncharacteristically un-compelling. He was racing through his sermon at a pace we had never witnessed before, and we all sat there unmoved, unengaged, even disinterested.

And then he stopped. He looked up from his notes and said, fighting a quiver in his voice, "I apologize for going so fast today and keeping it so close to the vest, but I'm afraid if I stop for even a moment I'm not going to make it." He was fighting emotion. It was clear he was experiencing tremendous sadness, and he was doing his best to keep it — and the accompanying tears — at bay.

And do you know what happened? As he launched back into his text, every person in that congregation began to cry, to sob, to weep. Why? Because this man, who meant so much to all of us, was struggling *not* to cry, was struggling *not* to lose it, and he wasn't succeeding. That was far more moving than any other possible sight.

Allow yourself to experience the emotions, and then, when it comes to the truly heightened emotions, the ones you wouldn't want other characters to witness, keep them at bay. That will be effective because it will be all too recognizable. So yes, when it comes to the big emotions, allow them, experience them, and then fight like the devil to keep them at arm's length.

Lesson 70:
Re-Experience, Don't Re-Create

I've got news for you. If you stop reading this book right now and are able to put the preceding pages into practice, you will experience genuine behavior on-stage. You will live truthfully in the moment. You will be present on-stage. It may happen in a rehearsal, it may happen in performance, but it will happen.

And so now I caution you.

Be careful.

Nothing feels better than that first time you experience truth as a character on-stage. It's the greatest high in the world for an actor. Because of that, when you're faced with that same scene the next night, be it rehearsal or performance, your natural tendency will be to "do the same thing." You're going to want to achieve that same truthfulness.

Be careful.

Be careful because your tendency will be to re-create what you did the previous evening, as opposed to starting over; your tendency will be to imitate what you did the night before, as opposed to setting up your circumstances all over again and *allowing* your character to experience what he experiences based on those circumstances. There are few things worse than an imitated performance (even if it's your own performance you're imitating). There are few things more un-engaging than a re-created event.

Instead, re-*experience* it. Savor the victory of living truthfully in the moment. Celebrate if you'd like. And then forget it. Start over again the next night. Remind yourself of the circumstances, of the wants, of the actions you will play to achieve the objectives, and allow yourself to experience what you experience.

I will never, ever forget when this first moment of truth happened to me. I was in college doing summer stock, and one night I had an emotional breakthrough. My character, who was going through a very disturbing period in his life, had to help a total stranger bury the stranger's dead son. My character was obviously moved by this experience, and one night during the run of the show, I, the actor, was genuinely moved as well. I felt something. I experienced truth. I really began to cry.

The audience was obviously moved, and afterwards my fellow actors congratulated me. I felt like I had succeeded as an actor. And I had.

But be careful.

The next night I didn't feel it so much, but I compensated by faking it, by forcing the tears and the trembling voice. The night after that I felt even less and forced even more. Same with the night after that and the night after that and so on, until one week after the best performance of my life, I was pushing. I was showing. I was indicating. In many ways, I was giving the *worst* performance of my life.

I was fortunate to have a director who understood exactly what was going on and who took me aside and said, "You know, your performance of that scene last week was amazing. It was really impressive. But I want to tell you that you don't need to re-create that. In fact, what you were doing with that moment before last week was also very effective, because it was *honest*." He looked me in the eye. "Just keep it honest. You don't need to cry on-stage for that moment to work. Just keep it honest."

And you know what? With that burden lifted off of me, without the *pressure* to "really feel it" each night, from that night on I was far more successful with that scene. Each night I set up my circumstances, reminded myself of what I wanted, and then I went for it. And some nights were amazing, but even the nights which weren't amazing, I am proud to say they were honest. And that's all any director (or playwright) can ask of you.

Enjoy the victory of a well-played scene, but don't fall into the trap of trying to re-create it each night. That will only lead to dismal acting. And no one likes that, right?

Lesson 71:
Be Surprised

One of the actor's greatest enemies in both rehearsal and performance is anticipation. It's so easy, once you're familiar with a script, to assume a certain inevitability with the play's events. "Of course my character makes that choice. What other choice would she make?"

This is very dangerous thinking.

Just as each day starts fresh in our lives, and we are faced with an assortment of choices, so must your character face each day in rehearsal and performance. You can't assume your character makes a certain choice. After all, aren't there other choices they could make? Nor should you assume that you will achieve the intentions the script says you will achieve. Conversely, you mustn't assume you will fail at certain objectives either. In other words, you must allow yourself to be surprised.

You need to start each performance and each rehearsal from point zero. Pretend that on this night the script has been re-written and you stand a real chance of getting what you want. Maybe your character is madly in love with a woman, and the play has her rebuffing him throughout. As an actor, you must never assume you will be rebuffed; you must face each rehearsal and performance with the hope that tonight will be different. Tonight you will get the girl. Otherwise, you will be anticipating the result, and eventually, once you're in the habit of anticipation, you won't truly be playing objectives. You won't truly be in the moment.

Put another way, remember that just because you've been rehearsing the material for four weeks and have grown accustomed to what is going on in the world of the play, this is all new stuff to an audience, and if you want them to enter the world of the play with you, you need to begin the play full of hope and expectation and not anticipate where the play is actually going.

The three sisters honestly think they'll get to Moscow. Romeo and Juliet have no doubt they'll find a way to get together. Willy Loman truly believes his sons will come to good. That's what makes these plays so wonderfully tragic; the protagonists have a set of expectations that aren't met. And if the actor can allow herself to be in a place where she isn't anticipating the end result, the audience can experience the character's journey as if it were their own.

But only if the actor doesn't anticipate and allows herself to be surprised.

Lesson 72:
Don't Break the Furniture

Actors love to break things. Props, chairs, desks, door units. If it's in a rehearsal room or on a stage, there's a good chance an actor will try his best to destroy it. Why? Because it's macho. It's intense. It's a feeling of accomplishment.

I have news for you. Nine times out of ten — ninety-nine times out of one hundred! — it's the actor who *doesn't* break the furniture who is far more interesting and believable.

Actors need to beware of intensity for the sake of intensity. It is a false, self-indulgent feeling that has more to do with therapy than acting. Actors need to resist feeling macho on-stage for the sake of feeling macho. Acting is an art, not a contact sport. And yet, far too many actors view acting as athletic therapy (or therapeutic athletics, take your pick) and so feel completely justified in destroying all props and set pieces while on-stage. By breaking furniture they feel as though they've really *acted*.

But think about it. How often do we break the furniture in our own homes? How often do we go to bars and restaurants, turning over chairs and tables, throwing glasses against the wall, breaking pool cues over our knees (or someone else's head)? If we're honest with ourselves, not often. Do those events happen? Sure, every once in a great while. But sometimes while watching scene work you get the impression that you *have* to throw and break things to truly be an actor. Nothing could be further from the truth.

I have no idea where the practice of breaking things in rehearsal and acting class started. But wherever it did, I'm here to tell you it's a good habit to break. Remember, the actor's task is to experience the emotion and then keep it at bay. An actor who throws beer mugs across the room is not keeping the emotion at arm's length. An actor who feels the need to turn over tables and chairs in every scene is playing the same tired emotion over and over — an emotion that appears only rarely in plays.

When many actors first start out, one of the things they love to do is be "intense." They look for intense roles, or worse, they look for ways to impose intensity on roles that don't call for intensity. They will inject screaming and shouting into a role, not because it's necessary, but because they can. Being intense feels satisfying. After a life of being polite and playing by the rules, it's very liberating to be in the theatre, where you can let it all out.

Be careful.

If the role doesn't call for that kind of intensity, if the play doesn't call for that emotion, it is a mistake to inject it. It will throw off the balance of what the playwright intended, and while it may feel "good" to be yelling on-stage, it will do nothing toward creating a believable evening of theatre. It may have more to do with serving yourself rather than serving the play.

Oh, it's fun to shout on-stage. It's a kick to swear. But beware the actor who is in love with intensity, who substitutes imagination with volume, who replaces nuance with bare emotion. There is a place for intensity on-stage. Definitely. And there are those rare moments when violent behavior is absolutely the appropriate choice, but make sure it's the right time and place for that kind of action. Otherwise, you'll fall into the trap of *showing* the audience how macho and intense you can be, which may feel oddly satisfying to you, but will only read as false behavior to an audience.

Lesson 73:
Acting Costs

Have you ever watched the Olympics, or the NBA Finals, or the Super Bowl? When those games are finished, the athletes have, as they say, "nothing left." They left it all out on the court (or the field or the pool). "I gave it 110%," they say in the locker room afterward, pleased that they're so spent. Well, let me tell you a little secret. When you're performing a major role in a play, it should be no different. It should cost you to perform that role. You should come into the wings afterwards drained emotionally, intellectually, maybe even physically. You should give it 110%.

You need to put your all into it and leave it on that stage. Each performance, each production. And if you ever come backstage after a performance and it didn't cost, you didn't do it right. A marathoner crossing the finish line should have nothing left. She should have used that final bit of energy with her kick on that home stretch. Performing a major role is no different. You should come across the finish line spent.

Acting costs. It exacts a price. The reason well-paid, serious actors make as much money as they do is because they're able to tap into feelings and expose them in front of others (on a regular basis, no less). The best actors are able to remember what it was like to be made fun of in kindergarten, remember the joy of a first kiss, remember the shame of embarrassment, remember, in short, every emotion and experience that they were subjected to in the grand, awful, wonderful, torturous years of their lives.

Throw yourself into it. Don't hold back. If this is what you love to do more than anything else, then why settle for mediocrity? Why allow yourself to just be okay? Why give just 80%? Or 90%? Or 100%?

Push yourself, bare yourself, allow yourself; just whatever you do, don't spare yourself. When acting costs, it works. And when it works, it satisfies both you and the audience.

Lesson 74:
Hide the Work

Are you sitting down? This is an important one.

Now that you've got some sense of how to work as an actor, now that you know what to do to improve your acting and make yourself more interesting on-stage, you must hide that work. You must disguise that technique.

Why? The reason is simple. Audiences do not come to the theatre to see actors at work; they come to see characters in action. They don't come to hear liquid U's and classic stage speech; they come to see characters engaged with other characters. They don't come to see actors making interesting and intellectual choices. They don't come to hear perfect scansion.

They come to watch a story as embodied by the characters in that story. That's all there is to it.

This is why there are so many terrific actors with little or no "training." They're naturals. They understand the simplicity that theatre requires (creating believable characters who interact with other believable characters in the context and style of the play), and they do their work accordingly.

But all too often "trained actors" feel the need to show their work. They spent all those years at NYU or Yale or Juilliard and paid an exorbitant amount to go there, so they're mighty sure they're going to make every agent, director, producer, and audience member see how "well trained" they are. They're going to show off their work.

Nothing could be more counter-productive. The last thing you want audience members to say to one another in the lobby after a performance is, "My, wasn't he a well trained actor?" No, you want them to say, "My, wasn't he a real heel?" Or "so charming?" Or "such a liar?"

The paradox is this: The actor must *hide* the work after going to the trouble — and expense — of *learning* the work. As an actor, you have to take classes, you have to read books, you have to attend rehearsals, so that everything is so ingrained in you that, in a very real sense, you forget it all. No one wants to see "technique"; audiences pay to see fully realized characters. Then you may well ask, "Why bother with learning altogether, since we're supposed to forget it as soon as we've learned it?" The answer is that some do skip the learning. Maybe they're naturals or they picked it up at an early age. More power to them. The vast majority of actors, however, need the help. They need to learn before they can forget.

You want to hide the work. You want to make it invisible. You want to cover up the seams. You want to give the impression that *you are this character* and that you've been typecast once again. (To me, there's nothing more satisfying than tricking the audience into thinking that I've been typecast.) In that way the audience won't be aware they're watching actors working, but will think instead they're watching characters in action. And that's what it's all about.

Sure, you've spent all this time in classes learning technique. Great! Now remember this: True technique is hiding that technique. The best technique is technique that's utterly invisible.

As the wonderful actress Lillian Gish once said, "Never get caught acting."

Amen.

Lesson 75:
Don't Forget to Play

Of all the things that can go wrong with actors and performances, this would have to go near the top of the list. Forgetting to play. And, ironically, it's the simplest of all the lessons.

Remember where your joy for theatre began? Was it doing plays in the basement for your parents? A pageant in junior high? The school musical in high school? Each of us has his or her own particular reasons for wanting to do theatre, and it began with some joyful spark way back when. Of course, over time, we learn technique (often to our undoing), get trained, hit a major market, and before we know it, there's no joy in our acting whatsoever. There's no play in the play; instead it's all very serious business.

A word of advice. *Don't forget to play.*

One of the great intangibles about a successful production is that there is an inherent joy in the performers. It's clear that they like what they're doing, be it a raucous comedy or a poignant drama. There is a sense of play in the performances that is genuine, affecting, and, not insignificantly, *contagious.* One of the reasons that high school productions are often so much fun (and so engaging) is not because the technique is good (it's usually quite awful), but because there's a strong sense of play among the performers. They enjoy what they're doing, and that goes a long way toward our enjoyment of it as well.

It's such a shame when actors lose that play — when acting becomes all too serious. Because you know what? That's partly the reason we are drawn to the theatre in the first place: To see performers *play.* Yes, we want to watch the story unfold, and sure, it's fun to have nice scenery and costumes to look at, but if there's no play from the actors, the result will oftentimes be an un-engaging mess — a self-righteous exercise in showing off.

So again: *Don't forget to play.*

Lesson 76:
Don't Forget the Audience

There are three ingredients to making theatre happen: a story, actors to tell the story, and an audience to tell the story to. If you leave out any of those elements, it is no longer theatre.

So why do we continually insist on forgetting the audience?

One of the great movements in contemporary theatre (especially in academic theatre) is to say, "Forget about the audience. If they don't get it, they're just not appreciative audience members." We often talk *at* the audience, but not *to* the audience. We're so preoccupied with how important we are, or how innovative the play's concept is, or how good we are as actors now that we're *trained*, that we forget there's a paying audience who wants to be entertained.

Now don't misunderstand me. By saying "entertained," I'm not implying that everything needs to be presented at the lowest common denominator. On the contrary, entertainment can co-exist with enlightenment and education. Challenging avant-garde works can be incredibly compelling, but let us never forget, no matter the genre, there's an audience present — an audience who *paid* to see us perform.

Yes, as a director I like to challenge audiences, and one of the primary reasons why I do theatre is to "comfort the afflicted and afflict the comfortable." But that doesn't rule out entertaining them. In fact, I can always better achieve my goals if they are, indeed, entertained.

As Viola Spolin wrote in *Improvisation for the Theatre*, "The actor must no more forget his audience than his lines, his props, or his fellow actors!"

As you progress and improve as an actor, don't get so in love with your new artistry that you forget the audience. After all, they make up a full third of the essential ingredients for theatre to exist. So don't neglect them; on the contrary, they should be embraced.

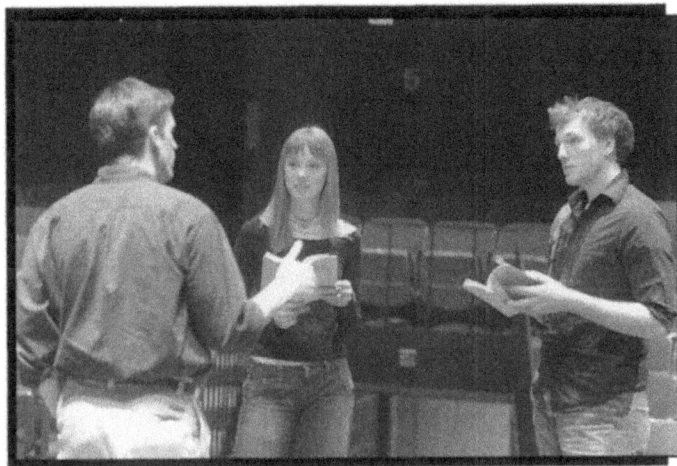

Tom Isbell, Annie Ragsdale, Andy Frye,

Photo by Brett Groehler
University of Minnesota-Duluth

Final Lessons

Lesson 77:
Learn from the Masters

One of the best classes I took in college was a poetry writing class, and it was wonderful for many reasons, not the least of which was the instructor, who was not only a published and nationally respected poet himself, but who knew how to teach others to write. His central credo in teaching poetry was simple: Learn from the masters. To that end we read every good poem by every good poet we could get our hands on. We then discussed what they had done and how they had done it so that we could improve our own writing. And it worked.

As an actor there are multiple ways to learn from the masters. A very obvious way is to attend good theatre and study good film. Watch what the best actors are doing. Model yourselves after them. I'm not suggesting you copy or steal (although that might happen subconsciously), but rather that you look to understand their choices and try to determine how they pulled them off. Notice nuance. Look for the subtleties. Examine the way they pursue actions. How do they seem to personalize? Study them. Learn everything you can from them.

When I say study good film, I don't just mean going to a movie and getting swept up in the story. I mean renting the movie and looking at it time and again, to the point where you're not distracted by the plot at all. Instead, your entire focus is on the actors and how they made those characters come to life.

This is called modeling, and there's probably no better way to learn. When Orson Welles made *Citizen Kane*, considered by many the greatest film ever made, he prepared by watching John Ford's 1939 film, *Stagecoach*, a total of forty times! (This, long before the days of VCRs.) When asked how he readied himself for directing, he replied that he studied the masters. When asked which masters, he answered, "John Ford, John Ford, John Ford."

The point is simple: Find the best actors on stage and screen and study them.

An even better way to learn from the masters is to act with them. At first, this might be you as a freshman working with an accomplished senior. Or it might be your first summer stock experience while still an undergraduate working with an Equity actor. Or maybe even working with a star when you're just starting out in film. No matter. Whatever the experience, learn everything you can from the master. Watch how they work, how they approach the role, their work habits, their focus and concentration. Be a sponge. Absorb everything that they do. If you're in a situation where you can talk with them, ask them questions, get their answers to how they approach the craft. Not how they got famous, but how they approach the craft. Chances are, they'll be flattered to share some secrets with an actor with such hunger for knowledge.

In the second film I ever did, I played the best friend of Robert DeNiro and Ed Harris, and it's no exaggeration to say I probably learned more from those two weeks than I did from a whole year of classes. Those two actors were (and still are) the masters of the craft, and I watched everything they did and how they did it. I soaked up everything I could.

Since Thespis emerged from the chorus 2,500 years ago and became "the first actor," certain actors have stood out over time and made a name for themselves. Don't let yourself think you're the first to make a go of this. On the contrary, give yourself the advantage of learning from the masters. Chances are, the masters themselves did it when they were younger, too.

Lesson 78:
Don't Compare

There are difficult lessons, and then there are *difficult lessons*. This may very well be the most difficult.

You're going to want to compare yourself to the actors around you: on TV, in rehearsal, in class. But I've got news for you; comparing does you absolutely no good. In fact, it does you a lot of harm.

As I said earlier, every actor is working on something different, so why bother comparing? Every actor is coming to a production (or a class) with an entirely different set of experiences, so why bother comparing? Every actor has different strengths and weaknesses, so why bother comparing?

It does you no good!

There is exactly one comparison that's okay to engage in. And that's with yourself. It's okay to compare where you are as an actor today with where you were last month, or last year, or five years ago. And if, after that comparison, you find you're not significantly better, maybe you should find another avenue to pursue. But if you realize you have made progress, good! Then keep believing you will continue to make progress, as long, of course, as you continue to work on improving.

But to compare yourself against other actors is silly — it's wasted time.

As a teacher, I see this all the time. When I return a grade sheet to a student with a half a page of criticism, that's criticism for that student only. I'm keyed in (I hope) to what each student needs to work on, and my criticism and grades are reflective of that particular student. Some students come in with natural abilities, and if I were to grade them purely on the same scale as their peers, they would have no difficulty in getting straight A's. But they wouldn't grow as actors. So I expect those who come in with such talents to grow as much as the novice actor who has a real spark but no discernible technique whatsoever.

But yet, when I return those grade sheets, I often see students crowding around each other, comparing grades and comments. Sure, it's always nice to get some idea of where you stand in comparison to your peers, but the best place to pick up on that is in casting. If you're constantly getting cast, you're probably doing something right. And if you're continually not getting cast, that needs to be a lesson for you as well.

When you're acting professionally, you may find it's difficult to read the trade magazines that list that week's casting notices because you continually see names other than your own. So you know what you do? You stop reading those trades, or at least those portions of the trades. If it gets you depressed when you read about other actors getting work, then stop reading about such things. Anything that gets in the way of your zone of confidence is harmful. Period.

I knew an actor who worked a great deal in television, but one thing he discovered was that he always did better at auditions if he was first (and the other actors hadn't arrived yet), or he was last (and the actors before him were already gone). He said he knew he wasn't really in competition with them — to give a good audition you are only in competition with yourself — but yet it helped him not seeing other actors, because then he wasn't even tempted to compare. He was able to trick himself into thinking that not only was he the only actor going up for the part, but he was the *best* actor going up for the part. And on those occasions when his audition wasn't at the beginning or the end, he said he couldn't help but look at the other actors (all his same type, but with better "builds, clothes and hair," he claimed) and it hurt his confidence — and his ability to give a good audition — tremendously.

Obviously, this was not the best situation for him, but at least he was aware of this shortcoming and would do everything he could to get around it.

To compare yourself with others does you absolutely no good. Compare yourself in the present with yourself in the past. That's the only comparison that helps.

Lesson 79:
Judge Not Lest Ye Be Judged

Pretty biblical for such a simple lesson.

If you haven't figured it out by now, you have plenty of things to work on as an actor. (If by some chance you have it all figured out and you're an acting god, then why the heck are you still reading this book?!?) So work on those things. And in the process, as you're focusing on what you need to do to better your own acting skills, don't worry about what others are working on.

You know, each actor is working on something different, something unique, each time he steps into a rehearsal room. It may be he or she is focusing on personalization that particular night, or on objectives, or on owning the character's gestures. Since this is all highly private stuff and you don't know (nor should you) what your fellow actors are working on, it behooves you not to judge. And wouldn't you rather they not judge you? After all, if you get the feeling from your fellow actors that you're all in this together, then you'll feel safe enough to make bold choices, to fail miserably, to keep experimenting.

Also, it's only natural that over time you'll be making friends with other actors. You'll meet them in school or in productions and you'll either keep in touch or just hear about what they're doing from others. A reminder: Be careful not to judge their choices. Some actors want to do commercials. Some Broadway. Some soap operas. Some regional theatre. Some community theatre. Who are we to judge and say that they're making a wrong choice? If it's what you want to do, go for it, and don't let anyone's judgment of you hold you back. To some people, film is the pinnacle of success. To others, it's doing a Chekhov at a regional theatre. To others still, it's doing six months on a cruise ship. Great.

There's no point judging others, because it's an entirely individual choice. And if you begin to judge others, you can only assume they're going to judge you. There's enough for you to concentrate on without wasting time evaluating and judging those around you. That's what a director is for. You just focus on yourself.

Lesson 80:
Avoid Attitude (Part Two)

Here's the other part to this lesson, which I first wrote about in **Classes and Rehearsals**. Not only does the lesson apply to your character's life on-stage, but to your own life off the stage as well. Although there are examples to the contrary, there is really no place in theatre or film for actors with attitude.

As you well know, you are always starting over as an actor. Every time you get cast you are faced with creating a new character, and although you might have enjoyed tremendous success in the past, there's no guarantee that will happen with each part in every play. Every time you step into a rehearsal hall for a first read-through you are all equal. Each actor has her part to play that is essential to the overall success of the production. Each actor is creating her role for the first time.

Based on that, why would anyone dare have attitude? And yet, of course, there are actors out there who somehow believe they are better than others. They have somehow convinced themselves they are higher up on the talent food chain. While it's true they might be higher up on the *business* food chain, that doesn't mean they'll stay there, nor does it mean they're the most talented.

I can see you reading this now, shaking your heads with disgust, thinking, "I will never be like this. I will never have attitude." And I hope it's true. But you would be surprised at how easy attitude comes. I have seen it on the college level where some actors have had the luxury of getting cast regularly, and they think themselves better than their peers. They may not be aware they have attitude, but it comes out. It shows itself in the little demands they make, in the comments they say ("I remember when I had the lead in the musical last year ..."), in how they get lazier and lazier in learning their lines ("Oh, I'll get them. I always do.") or getting to rehearsal on time.

I have seen attitude on the professional level, with actors who have just recently gotten their big break and now behave as if it was entirely expected, as if *of course* they have their own TV show, was there ever really any doubt? They are the ones who make it big and then fall in love with their income, their multiple homes, their status, *themselves*, and somehow forget about the work itself, becoming ensnared in a net of mediocrity.

But you know what's funny? The very best actors don't have attitude. The best actors know that luck was one of the things that got them where they are, and they realize the need to keep doing their homework if they're going to remain successful. The best actors recognize that they may be popular now, but fame is fleeting, and audience perceptions change. The best actors recognize that everyone is starting in the same place when it comes to beginning rehearsal or shooting a film. The best actors realize the work that's involved in being the best.

My first film was with the great Anne Bancroft, and the director called some informal rehearsals a week before we began shooting. Four of us sat around a table — Ms. Bancroft, the director, the actress playing my wife, and me — and the director said, "Ms. Bancroft, would you like to tell these actors anything?"

She looked aghast and said, "Oh no, I'm in the same place they are: Trying to figure out my character." This from an actress who had won both an Academy Award and a Tony Award.

But she is not the only one. The reputations of the *best* actors and actresses is that they cop no attitude. They understand the nature of the business, they understand the work they need to do to create a believable character, they understand their own luck that brought them there, and they understand that everyone is truly in the same boat, even if some have far more experience than others.

It's tricky, of course. As Laurence Olivier pointed out, it's a difficult equation actors must work out for themselves, because they need two things to be successful. "One is confidence, absolute confidence," Olivier said, "and the other an equal amount of humility towards the work." That's a tough balance to find.

But there's simply no place for attitude among actors. Not on the high school level, not on the collegiate level, not in the professional world. Period.

Thus endeth the sermon.

Lesson 81:
Work on Your Body

If you're serious about becoming an actor you need to be serious about working on your body. I'm not saying you need to hire a personal trainer and enter the Olympics as a weightlifter. I am saying you need to pay attention to your body and do what you need to do so you're accentuating your type to your best ability and so you're in good enough shape to handle any role.

First, about type. If you're a leading man or woman, you need to be in shape. Whether it's fair or not, part of the reason we go to the theatre and film is because we like to look at beautiful people. If you're a leading man, it makes no sense for you not to be working out. You need to be fit. You need to be "watchable." That doesn't mean you need to look like Stallone or Schwarzenegger; it just means you need to be fit. (If you want to look like Ahh-nold, that's your own prerogative.)

If you're a character actor, it's maybe not as big a deal that you're fit. In fact, it may work against you if your type is the "heavy sidekick." But you still need to be in good enough shape that you have more options and versatility in playing roles. Some of the classics, especially, demand great stamina to perform, and if you're not in shape to pull them off, you're only hurting yourself. Falstaff, for example, is a demanding role, and woe to the actor who isn't in good enough shape to pull it off.

In addition to being in shape, there's also the issue of body control. That's why movement classes are so important, whether they're dance, Tai Chi, stage combat, tumbling, whatever. Anything that works on your body awareness, control, flexibility, and strength can only feed you as an actor. In the first place, you won't be confined to just doing what your own persona does; you'll have a physical vocabulary that will let you alter your body from performance to performance so you're not stuck doing the same old thing. Secondly, you'll stretch your own personal boundaries and have more range with the roles you play best.

If you're serious about acting, *please* work on your body. Not just for your sake, but for the audience's.

Lesson 82:
Speak the Speech

As with the body, so with the voice. Voice work (and I'm not talking about singing here) is important for an actor for many reasons, not the least of which is the fact that the voice is connected to the emotion. Don't think of voice as these sounds you create; rather, voice is connected to impulse and emotion, and by freeing it, you're freeing feelings. By working on your voice, you're actually getting in touch with your inner impulses. (Kristen Linklater's book, *Freeing the Natural Voice*, is, perhaps, the best at making this concept clear.)

Also, very obviously, voice work can help rid you of certain vocal problems you may have, whether they be guttural stops, an annoying nasality, a consistent hoarseness, or whatever plagues you. A good voice teacher will not only instruct you how to use your voice properly, but will connect it to the rest of your body.

In addition to voice, there is the matter of speech, both your own and the character's. The first reason to work on speech is to clean up your own manner of speaking and to rid yourself of any regionalisms (dialects) that you may have. Don't worry; just because you're being taught how to free yourself from these regionalisms doesn't mean you're selling your soul. If you think your southern accent is your bread and butter, there's no reason why you have to lose it entirely. But you do need to learn to rid yourself of the regionalism if you want to have some versatility in playing roles. (Juliet with a Southern accent in a New York Shakespeare in the Park production would probably be fairly comical.)

Speech work is also valuable for learning dialects, especially the two important ones: Southern and British. Yes, if you get cast you will no doubt have a coach working with you on the dialects, but there are two strong reasons to learn dialects as soon as you can. The first is because it will help you get the job in the first place if you're already comfortable with the dialect; the director won't be reluctant to cast you in a production of Shaw if you have already mastered a British dialect. It's one less thing for her to worry about in rehearsal.

Also, and perhaps more importantly, when first learning a dialect, the new way of speaking acts as a barrier — another layer — between the actor and his impulses. The more comfortable you are with the dialect, the more it becomes part of you, so if you have learned the major dialects *before* you go into a show, you won't be struggling with phonetics and sounds when you should be working on character.

The more you address voice and speech *before* getting cast in a play, the more prepared and better off you'll be. If you do the work now, you won't have to do it later.

Lesson 83:
Don't Make Excuses

A life in the theatre is a life of rejection. You experience it at every level: From high school and college when you don't get the lead in the play, to your life as a professional actor in a major market where you're not cast nearly as often as you'd like. Being an actor means dealing with rejection, and the sooner you come to terms with this the better.

I am constantly amazed at the number of actors who don't see this coming, who seem to think they are above the rejection that others experience. Don't they realize that *every* actor experiences rejection? Even Katharine Hepburn, who won four Academy Awards, experienced it. She was panned by the New York critics for some of her early stage performances. (In one review, Dorothy Parker said she "ran the gamut of emotion from A to B.") Even after winning an Academy Award, she was considered "box office poison." But do you know what she did about it? She continued to make smart choices as an actor. She continued to work at her craft. She continued to improve. She didn't whine, she didn't moan. She took an active, positive approach to her rejection, acting until the last years of her life.

Laurence Olivier received terrible reviews early in his career. About his Romeo, the London *Evening News* wrote: "Mr. Olivier can play many parts; Romeo is not one of them. His blank verse is the blankest I've ever heard." But he continued to believe in himself. He didn't make excuses for his performances; instead, he kept at his craft until he won the respect of the critics and the public alike.

If you're in college and you're not getting cast, you have several choices. One is to leave that school. After all, maybe the teachers there don't know what they're talking about. Maybe they don't truly appreciate the gifts you have as an actor. That's one choice. The other is let yourself truly listen to what they're saying and begin seriously working on those elements of your acting that are preventing you from getting cast. In other words, what if what they're saying is right? Wouldn't it be nice to address those issues sooner rather than later?

Whatever you do, there's one thing you should not, can not, *must* not do: Make excuses. It gets you absolutely nowhere and will eventually begin to make you all the more bitter and frustrated, which in turn makes you all the more difficult to cast. Once you start making excuses, you give directors and producers reasons not to cast you. Think about it from their perspective: Who would you rather work with? Someone with strengths and weaknesses as an actor who accepts responsibility for their actions and is willing to work on their faults, or someone with strengths and weaknesses who would rather make excuses for why they're not the next best thing?

As the old joke goes, how can you tell when a plane is full of actors? Answer: When the engine stops, the whining continues.

All you do by making excuses is let yourself wallow in your own self-pity. Life's too short for that, and there's far too much work to be done on improving yourself as an actor to waste time feeling sorry for yourself. Yes, it's disappointing when you don't get cast, or when you don't get cast how you'd like to be cast. Sure, you're allowed to feel that disappointment. That's more than fair. But then it's time to go on. Be gracious in defeat. Learn from your mistakes. And be all the more determined to succeed on the next occasion. That's the kind of actor I want to work with. And that's the kind of actor who works consistently.

Lesson 84:
Avoid Green Rooms

It's fun to talk to other actors because, in this whole, vast world of six billion people, they are the ones — the proud, the few — who understand what you're going through. Why? Because they're going through it themselves. And so it's comforting to gripe about directors and classes and auditions and not getting cast with people who understand. You can try to have these conversations with people outside of the theatre, but they don't really understand. Not really. Actors understand. And besides, misery loves company.

Okay. Fair enough. But a warning:

Green rooms are the devil. Green rooms are satanic. Green rooms are the antichrist.

Well, okay, maybe I exaggerate slightly, but green rooms are breeding grounds for discontent. Instead of being places where actors share and grow and thrive, green rooms often become places of discontent and unhappiness. You might have been perfectly happy in an acting class or at rehearsal, but now that you hear others around you complain you see that they have a point, and before you know it you're chiming in to the conversation with your own examples and gripes.

I can't tell you how dangerous this is, and you know why? Although you won't be aware of it, you'll bring that attitude into a class or rehearsal with you. Once you become a part of the green room culture, it's all too easy to be a complainer and not a do-er, to be someone "who isn't getting his fair share," as opposed to someone who's making things happen for himself. Part of the reason for this is because the people who like to live in the green rooms are the very people who have the most time to live there: the un-cast, for example. And it gives them power to hang out in the green room and bring others down. If they're not having a good experience in the theatre, why should the people around them?

Have you heard this one? How many actors does it take to screw in a light bulb? One hundred. One to screw it in, the other ninety-nine to say they could have done it better.

Well, that's what green rooms are like.

This is not to say that talking with other actors is not beneficial. On the contrary. It's just that there are certain places where talking can become complaining, and that does no one any good.

Complaining leads to inaction, it leads to self-pity, it leads to an "attitude." Trust me, given the choice, directors would do anything rather than hire actors with attitude, and teachers recognize that there is no greater hurdle for actors to get over than a wall of attitude.

Lastly, when I say avoid green rooms, it bears mentioning that green rooms aren't just in green rooms. They can be in diners, apartments, even rehearsals themselves when not on-stage. Any place where actors come to gripe is a potential green room. Be above the green room mentality. Remember, you're striving to be an artist. As artists, it's more than acceptable to be frustrated with the system of getting work, but keep your complaining to a minimum. If you're not careful, you'll become one of those actors who thrive on making the lives of others as miserable as his own.

Lesson 85:
Take What You're Given

Who doesn't want to be the leading man or woman in a film? Who wouldn't want to be a major Broadway star? What television actor wouldn't want to be on a successful sitcom that runs a dozen years, where each day on the set is a gift of laughter and good work?

Unfortunately, not everyone can experience those dreams. For the vast majority of actors, acting has a far different reality. And you know what? That's okay.

All too often I see young actors who desperately want to be leading men or women when they're just not leading men or women types. Why do they want to be the leads? Because they grew up idolizing Julia Roberts or Tom Hanks or Denzel Washington or Meryl Streep, and they want "to be like them." Sorry to say, not everyone can be like them. You can strive to better yourself as an artist, to have that level of talent and commitment to your craft, but there's no guarantee you will have that kind of career.

Why? Because you just may be a very different type. Or you may not get the lucky break to leap from your current acting status to that elevated status.

To that I say, it's okay. Make the most of your life wherever you are, whatever you do. Strive to improve as an actor in whatever genre you're working, in whatever community you're living. Take what you're given and make the most of it. Please don't waste your life pining for the unattainable. Be where you are. Accept your circumstances, and try to be the very best actor you can be in that place, at that time.

This is not to say that you can't dream, that you should stop trying, that you should just throw up your hands and say, "This is it. I'm stuck at this level for the rest of my professional life." Not at all. But I am suggesting you take an *honest* appraisal of yourself — your type, your talents, your overall situation — and work from there. If you're not truly a leading man or woman, then please stop trying to market yourself as one. You can't smash a square peg in a round hole, and yet that's exactly what many actors spend their lives doing.

One of the best character actresses I know told me that she spent the first two years of college thinking she was a leading woman, and being insulted when she was even called back for the character roles. Finally, in her junior year, it dawned on her that she was not only a character actress, but a really good character actress, and the work she did from that point on was incredible. It was amazing. She created some of the most memorable roles on those stages, and her only regret was that she hadn't come to that realization sooner.

I myself remember auditioning for a play as a college freshman, going up against not only upperclassmen but graduate students as well. At the audition I got to choose which role I was auditioning for, and, of course, I chose the lead. It didn't matter that I wasn't really the right type. It didn't matter that I didn't yet have the experience (or the talent) to pull off the lead of a major play on the main stage of a major university. I was conditioned from high school to want "the lead." After the audition the director asked me, "So why do you want this role?"

"It's the lead," I answered, as if nothing could be more obvious. I saw from his amused reaction that I had much to learn.

He cast me, not in the lead, but in a tiny supporting role, which grew into a larger role when another actor had to drop out. The production itself was a terrific experience, and I ended up working for that director off and on for the next twenty years, not because I was the lead the first time he saw me act, but because I took what I was given, made the most of it, and eventually earned his respect.

What I have come to learn is that you need to take what you're given. If you're not the lead, accept that. If you're qualified for another role, accept that. Don't try to force something that isn't there. It may be that you're more suited for a life on the stage, even though you'd really rather do TV. It may be you're more suited for a life on TV, even though you'd really rather do film. Whatever.

Take what you're given. Yes, work, work, work to improve yourself, and no, you shouldn't completely abandon your dreams. But do be honest with yourself. Accept the good things around you and go with them.

Lesson 86:
Bloom Where You're Planted

My high school Sunday School teacher was a gregarious Texas woman who demanded a lot from her students and gave even more in return; everyone whose life she touched was better for it. A dozen or so years after graduating from high school, I moved to Los Angeles from New York. My career was going well enough; I had been a regular on a TV series, done a movie, was landing guest spots fairly regularly.

But.

I wasn't taking to L.A. I missed my friends in New York, I missed the vibrant theatre community there, I missed that portion of my life. So when my former Sunday School teacher came to town and we got together, she saw me moping and whining, longing for my life in New York. And being the blunt Texas woman that she is, she told me straight up to bloom where I was planted. In other words, I was living in L.A., I had made that choice, I may as well make the most of it. Otherwise I was just shooting myself in the foot, and I would bring that negative energy into the audition room with me.

What great advice.

Once she told me that, I began to accept — and even embrace — my life in Los Angeles. I became active in founding a theatre company. I began jogging along the ocean. I began working out again. I took control of auditions. And suddenly, I was working more. A lot more.

Go figure.

All it took was an awareness of what I was doing and a few simple adjustments, and I was back in business. It was that easy. Suddenly I was blooming where I was planted.

I see inexperienced actors struggle with this. On the college level they may have difficulty accepting the differences between this particular program and the way some other program is run. Or they don't like the casting policies. Or the choice of shows. Or the classes. You know what? If you make the decision to be a student there, accept that. Embrace it. Does that mean you can't make or suggest changes? Absolutely not. But don't let it get in the way of your own growth as an artist in the theatre.

Young actors also struggle with this notion when they first move to a big market. Maybe they're wondering if they should have moved to Chicago instead of New York, or vice versa. Or maybe they can't find an acting teacher they trust. Or maybe they don't like "the system." You know what? Bloom where you're planted. Embrace the city you're in. Accept the way it's run. And *enjoy* being a part of the process. Don't just tolerate it; relish in it.

The actors who thrive are those who give the appearance of loving life, of loving the city they're in, of loving theatre. That kind of energy is wonderfully contagious, and directors, casting directors, and producers pick up on it in a second. That's the kind of actor they want to hire. Not the shy or disgruntled one, but the one who is embracing the opportunity to be young and alive and auditioning.

Wherever you are, wherever you go, embrace that place and those experiences. Bloom!

Lesson 87:
Make Your Own Luck

I firmly believe that you need some amount of luck to find success as an actor. The fact is, there are so many thousands and thousands of actors out there, all trying to attain the same goals that it's only natural that some (many!) good actors are left in the dust. This is the sad truth. After all, there are only so many good roles and there are *many* actors worthy of playing those roles.

So does this make you angry? After all, you've just spent four years getting your BFA and another three on your MFA only to find out that you need a third degree: Namely, luck. Be not discouraged, and here's why: Good actors make their own luck. The actor who earned both a BFA and an MFA, for example, is making her own luck, because that actor is not only developing technique (and thereby increasing her casting potential), but the chances are that that actor will make contacts through at least one of those programs, contacts that might have lucrative payoffs down the road. There might even be an actor showcase in a major market at the end of the MFA training. These events lead to so-called "lucky breaks."

Golfing legend Gary Player said it best, claiming that golf is a game of luck. "The harder I practice," he said, "the luckier I get."

You make your own luck. You don't sit around waiting to be discovered, you lead an active life as an actor, performing as much as you can, meeting as many people as you can, working as professionally as possible, and by so doing you are creating opportunities where you will impress one person who will give you the job that will catapult you to the next level. Outsiders may see this as a lucky break; you and you alone will understand the years of toil and sacrifice that were necessary to reach that moment. Luck rarely shows up on your doorstep unannounced. You work for it. You create situations where it can thrive. And when it does magically appear, you're ready for the opportunity.

People who sit around hoping luck will strike aren't really expecting luck; they're expecting a miracle. Miracles come out of nowhere. You make your luck.

Even though I strongly believe that luck is a crucial element in the successful actor's makeup, I just as strongly believe that it's a cultivated ingredient. It's one you can create, foster, nurture.

The more you work, the luckier you'll get. I'm sure of it.

Lesson 88:
Beware of Talk

As you proceed along in your development as an actor, you will find it enjoyable — necessary even — to stop along the way to talk about your craft. Fine. But one word of warning: A little bit of talk goes a long way.

There is nothing so discouraging as a roomful of young actors sitting around discussing their "art" if they then do nothing concrete about it. There is nothing so depressing as listening to actors in a green room discuss their "art" when they should be on the stage or in the classroom working on their craft. Art comes as a byproduct of craft. Work on your craft, and art will follow.

While I think it's both necessary and important to discuss elements of the craft along the way — after all, you gain insights and strengths from those around you going through the same experiences — a little bit goes a long way. Don't let talk be a substitute for work. As an actor, you have work to do. Talk is fine and even beneficial, and infinitely easier than getting on your feet, but ultimately, it's the work that will make your fortune as an actor.

Use the talk to motivate you. Let the talk inspire you. Don't let it serve as a replacement for what you need to do to work on yourself or your character.

Don't just talk about art. Create it.

Lesson 89:
Check Your Egos at the Door

Back in January of 1985, a number of the world's most popular singers gathered one evening to record the song, "We Are the World," to benefit United Support of Artists for Africa. It seemed as though nearly every major musician of the time was there: Bruce Springsteen, Michael Jackson, Billy Joel, Ray Charles, Bette Midler, Diana Ross, Paul Simon, Willie Nelson, Tina Turner, Bob Dylan, Stevie Wonder, and many, many more. It was a staggering collection of talent, all there to sing a song to help raise funds for a good cause. They gathered under cover of darkness at a studio in Los Angeles, and Quincy Lewis, the organizer behind the event, had gone to great lengths to make it happen. Because his one concern was how these high-profile stars would interact, he did a very smart thing. He placed a sign above the door where all the celebrities entered. The sign read, "Check your egos at the door."

With that simple mantra he had made his point. This wasn't your typical rock event with people waiting on the stars hand and foot. This wasn't about dressing rooms and catered food. It was about putting a song together that would raise funds and awareness for the starving people of another continent. When the stars came and passed under the sign, they got the message, and it was reportedly one of those amazing events where all these extremely talented singers (with extremely healthy egos) got together and also got along.

Because they checked their egos at the door.

Personally, I believe we should post such signs over the door of every acting classroom and every rehearsal hall in the country because there is nothing more destructive than egos. Egos can tear apart a rehearsal or an actor's growth. Contrary to high school behavior, plays aren't about who has the most lines or who gets the most laughs. Plays are about the event that the play is dramatizing, and each actor somehow serves that message. It may be a small role, it may be a large role, it may be a serious role, it may be a comic role. The point is that each actor is essential to make the thing run, and if egos are left out of the equation, there is a far better chance for overall success.

Acting classes aren't about who's better or worse. Acting classes are about assessing your individual strengths and weaknesses and working on what needs working on. So another actor is funnier than you are? Big deal. So another actor is better at accessing their emotions? What does it matter to you? What matters is where you are as an actor and what steps you're taking to improve. If you leave your ego at the door so as not to get bruised by other actors' strengths, then you'll give yourself a chance to grow. Similarly, if you're an actor of considerable strength (or an actor comfortable with your character) it behooves you not to impede another actor's progress. Whether you know it or not, you need that rehearsal (or class) just as much as any other actor. You may be working at a higher level, but an actor's work is never done. It's often the actor with the native talent who doesn't cultivate that talent who gets passed by. I can't tell you the number of times I have witnessed "the tortoise and the hare" in acting classes, where the lazy actor with the innate talent is soon passed by the actor with less innate talent but who works hard to compensate for that lack.

One of my favorite actors in class was not only one of the most talented, but also the most supportive. He was head and shoulders above the other actors around him, but you wouldn't have known it by his actions. He was so enthusiastic in his peers' growth that those students progressed at a rate unlike any class I've ever had. Why? Because he left his ego at the door. And when he came to rehearsal, he was the first to climb up on-stage and say, "Let's get to work."

There is no place for ego in an acting classroom or a rehearsal hall. Whether you're accomplished or not, it can only stifle you. Check it at the door.

Lesson 90:
Relieve Pressure

Let's be up front about this. Acting is a life of monotony, sometimes even boredom, punctuated by moments of intense pressure: the big audition, the first time the camera settles on your face for the close up, opening night. These are pressure-filled moments, and the successful actor is someone who has learned how to handle such events. If you let the situation win, if you let nerves get the better of you and stifle your impulses and natural creative flow, chances are your professional life will be limited.

But it need not be. All you need to do is adjust your mindset so that you don't merely *endure* pressure situations, you *prevail*. You rise above those moments when everything is on the line, allowing yourself to do the work you need to do, shutting out any distraction that takes you out of the moment.

The best athletes understand this. They want to be in the pressure situations. They want the basketball when down by two points with two seconds left. They want to come to bat in the bottom of the ninth with two outs and the bases loaded. They want to be quarterback for the two-minute drill when their team is down by a touchdown. In any case, they want to be the one on the line in the final moments of the game.

Part of the best athletes' ability to perform in those moments, as voiced by baseball reliever Tom Gordon, is their ability to focus on that one thing at that one moment. Focus on that one pitch, or that one swing of the bat. Don't think an inning or two ahead. Don't think about any mistakes earlier in the game. Think about the present, and about the present only.

Gordon also pointed out that the great players have fun. They enjoy what they're doing, they continue to have fun, so that when they're placed in so-called pressure situations, they don't see them as pressure situations. They see them as opportunities to prove themselves and to grow.

That's what actors need do as well. Find those opportunities to grow and embrace them. Forget that it's opening night; focus instead on achieving your objectives. Disregard the fact that it's your first close up in a film. Instead, think of what a wonderful opportunity you're given, the camera close on your face, or the audition which could send your career in a new direction. What a gift you've been given. You then owe it to yourself to treat yourself right by eliminating the pressure itself, and focus instead on the work at hand. Don't think about the possible Academy Award. Don't let yourself think about the potential salary boost. Do think about pursuing your objective. Do think about being in the moment.

In this way, much of the pressure will be eliminated of its own accord.

Lesson 91:
Acting Isn't Therapy

I hate to have to write this, and I only do so because every once in a great while I see an actor — or at least someone who *pretends* to be an actor — misuse the notion of what theatre is all about.

Theatre is a means to entertain. It is a chance to publicly explore an issue, to make an audience laugh, or be afraid, or think, or cry. It is created collaboratively, with a playwright creating a script, which is then interpreted by a director, who passes that directorial concept onto a team of actors and designers. This group of actors plays their characters with the intention of bringing the play's message to life. That's their job. To do that, of course, they need to be skilled enough to be convincing in their moments of comedy, in their moments of tragedy, and everything in-between. That's what an actor does.

What an actor should avoid is using the theatre — or even the acting classroom — as a place to vent her repressed emotions.

Acting isn't therapy. That's not its purpose. Because acting costs, it's very possible that you will feel a certain catharsis after playing certain characters, and that's perfectly fine. In fact, it's more than fine. What isn't fine, and must be avoided, is playing the emotion for the sake of playing the emotion. What isn't fine, and must be avoided, is using a character to simply get your own personal stuff off your chest. You shouldn't use the rehearsal room or the stage as a private therapy session. Remember, the goal is for the truthful playing of the scene; it's not about your own personal gains.

The former is laudatory and what the theatre is all about. The latter, I'm ashamed to say, is self-indulgent. It is strictly for your benefit at the cost of everyone around you. That should be avoided at all costs.

If you're unclear on the dividing line between the two, a good teacher or director will be your guide, and you should be working with a good teacher or director if you're venturing into your own personal emotion.

If you want to go to therapy — and personally, I would recommend that every actor do — then that's something that takes place on your own. Not during class or rehearsal time, and certainly not during performance.

Lesson 92:
Honor the Three Rules of Improv

In this day and age, most every actor has had some experience with improvisation. Maybe it's in an exercise in class, maybe it's in rehearsal. And chances are you'll continue to have other experiences with improv as you continue along in your quest to be a working actor. So. Here are some tips on how to approach and what to get from improv so that it's a fruitful experience for you.

For better or worse, most actors' impressions of improv are of the comedic nature — *Second City* or *Whose Line Is It Anyway?* — and there are certainly some very gifted actors who make their living doing this very type of thing. However, the majority of improv that most actors will do as they prepare a character or work on expanding their own personal boundaries, has very different goals. In those cases, more often than not, the intention is to find truth: either the character's or your own. It's not about making someone laugh. It's not about the odd funny line. It is about being truthful on-stage, which for many actors, is a new experience.

With that in mind, there are three basic "rules" you should follow if you want to get the most out of your improv experiences.

Number 1: Don't entertain. This is counter to comedy improv, where the supreme goal is to make people laugh and show them a good time. But with improv that stretches you as an actor and/or develops your belief system as a character, the last thing you want to do is entertain. Far from it. Instead, you want to focus on your objectives, your feelings, and your awareness of the surroundings. You want to explore relationships with the other characters, pursue actions, and discover how your character walks, sits, talks, moves. You want to start building a *history* for your character. None of this — not one bit! — has anything to do with entertaining. The moment you start to want to entertain (your classmates, your director, your teacher) is the moment that the improv will begin to be worthless.

Improv of this nature isn't about the funny line. It isn't about saying or doing the outrageous thing. It is about being fully in the moment, and you can't be in the moment if you're thinking like a playwright and trying to come up with the next comic line. Improv of this nature is about trust: trust in the work you've done and seeing where it takes you as you play your objectives and explore relationships.

And do you know the most ironic thing of all? By not wanting to entertain, you will be incredibly entertaining. Incredibly so. At times even funny. Not because you're coming up with Neil Simon-like comic lines, but because you're playing the reality of the situation, and when an audience sees actors playing truth and *recognizing* that truth, there is absolutely nothing more entertaining to watch. It can be moving, funny, poignant, whatever. Nothing is more watchable than truthful improv. And nothing is deadlier than improv that is supposed to be truthful but is instead *trying* to be entertaining.

Many actors blanch when they learn they're going to do improvisations, either in class or rehearsal, and the reason is usually because they think they're going to have to entertain. "I'm not funny," they say.

My answer to them is, "Good." Then they'll probably have a better chance of not *trying* to be funny. Improv of this nature is really very easy, and the biggest obstacle is the desire on the part of some actors to consistently entertain. That's not what this improv is about. On the contrary: Don't entertain.

Second rule: Don't show. Because improv of this nature is usually employed at an early stage of rehearsal, many actors find it tempting to want to show what they're working on, or they want to show the circumstances. Don't. Fight that urge. Again, it will be far more truthful, and therefore beneficial, if you resist that particular temptation. As we've discussed earlier in this book, we *show* very little in our real lives. We *experience* much. Your goal as an actor in an improv (as an actor in a role) is to experience the elements around you, not to show them. The showing will take care of itself by your experiencing them.

The last rule is the perfect rule, meaning this: Whatever anyone says is perfect. If another character says to you, "Are you feeling better today?" then you can rightly assume you were feeling worse yesterday. What they say becomes fact — it's perfect — and you can't deny it. This is actually a much easier way to work. Instead of having to invent a mountain of circumstances, you need only pay attention to what the other characters in the scene are giving you. In this way, you begin to rely on the other actors, you begin a process of give-and-take, you connect with them. And this may well have been the sole intention of the improv all along.

Don't entertain. Don't show. And all is perfect. Follow these precepts, and you will be far more successful with improv than you might have expected to be.

Lesson 93:
Ask for the Teacup

There's an old saying in the theatre that "Dying is easy; comedy's hard."

Truer words were never spoken. It's one thing to do a comedy in a small community for your friends and family; it's another to do it on a larger scale for an audience of strangers.

Comedy is demanding. It requires timing. It requires a sense of truth, but also a heightened degree of reality. Comedy is not funny if it's not somehow based on reality — what makes comedy so funny is its recognition factor, after all — but then again, if it's "too serious," it won't be funny either. Comedy is walking a tightrope, and there's probably no better way to get good at it than through practice, both on-stage and off.

There's a famous story of Laurence Olivier doing a Noel Coward play, and early on in the run Olivier said a line having to do with a teacup that got a terrific laugh. The next night he tried to say the line the same way and got less of a laugh. The next night he again tried to go back to that original line reading and got even less of a response. And so on, until finally he was not getting any laugh at all. At which point he asked Mr. Coward what he was doing wrong. Coward replied, "My dear boy, ask for the teacup, not the laugh."

In other words, if you consciously go for the laugh, you won't get it. But if you maintain that balance of realism with a slightly heightened sense that comedy requires, you will produce the required response.

One of the smartest observations on how to play comedy comes from *The Director's Eye* by John Ahart. Ahart points out that in comedy "the world is out of control. Things go too fast … and then faster." In other words, the actor shouldn't try to *be funny*; he should just try to catch up with the world around him.

Noel Coward firmly believed that playing comedy was more difficult than playing an emotional role in a serious play. In the latter instance, actors have the advantage of letting the emotion carry them through, but in a comedy the actor has to continually keep herself in check. As Coward said: "If the dialogue is good, let the dialogue speak. Don't wink. Don't make faces. Don't try to make it funny."

In other words, ask for the teacup, not for the laugh.

Lesson 94:
Fear Not Shakespeare

The great actor John Carradine once said, "If you can play Shakespeare, you can play anything."

And yet it seems as though most young American actors are afraid of Shakespeare. Because they don't understand much of the vocabulary, because they don't speak with a British accent, and because it seems productions of Shakespeare are always on a pedestal, they're afraid of failing.

It needn't be like this.

It's true that Shakespeare uses words that most of us don't incorporate in our daily lives, but it's no big deal to look up words and discover what he's saying. It's true also that some sentences may not be immediately clear, but that also can be solved rather easily with a little application. The main obstacle for young actors is fear, and it's a fear simply because they haven't done Shakespeare before. Once you've performed him, his plays become much more accessible. In fact, most actors agree that it's easier to learn Shakespearean lines because the rhythm is written into the text for you.

One of the great pleasures in an actor's life is playing the great roles of Shakespeare. Why? Because he gives you so much to work with. Not only is the language far superior to any other playwright's, but he writes complex characters who need that heightened language to express what they want to say.

Of course, that very heightened language is the very thing that scares many actors, and it shouldn't. The trick in mastering Shakespeare is actually very simple; it takes some work, yes, but it's simple nonetheless.

The first thing you need to learn is scansion, the metric rhythm of the verse. Some directors have actors follow the rhythms religiously; others have you work against it. The important thing for actors to know is what the rhythms are, so you're not fighting them one way or the other. Although it's a dangerous word to use, Shakespeare's texts are *poetry*, and you need some understanding of scansion and how the rhythm breaks down to properly play the text.

Scansion is the first place where Shakespeare gives you the clues to his characters. As you know, most of his verse is in iambic pentameter (five feet of two syllables each, each line with essentially the same rhythmic pattern — duh DA duh DA duh DA duh DA duh DA), but occasionally he will intentionally change the scheme, either making it fewer than five feet or longer, or changing the rhythm so it's not completely iambic. (In other words, instead of duh DA, it becomes DA duh, or DA DA.)

How does this change in rhythm help you as an actor, you ask? It's a signal. It's a signpost on a map. It's Shakespeare's way of telling you that something is going on with the character at that particular moment. Maybe the character is flustered, maybe she's in love, maybe she's trying to make an important point, maybe she's lying. Whatever. There's no strict translation that this means that and that means this, but it's your job as an actor to decipher Shakespeare's clues and figure out what's going on in the character's head at that moment.

It's a puzzle, and the playwright is leaving you clues.

Another difference in acting styles is in terms of physicality, mainly because the costumes are so different from modern day dress (unless the director is deliberately choosing to set it in contemporary time). This difference in clothing, as much as anything, dictates a different type of movement within the clothes. A woman wearing a corset and long, flowing dress will no doubt move differently than when she's wearing jeans. The same goes for a man wearing tights and a doublet, with a rapier and dagger on his belt. Actors today tend to behave very naturalistically on-stage, due in part to the large influence of film. Sad to say, that style doesn't always work with Shakespeare, which is not so realistic, but rather requires a heightened sense of language and physicality.

That's not to say there aren't elements in common. Actors still need to do their homework. They still need to determine circumstances, wants and actions, and need to be able to play them effectively. (Don't get in the habit of letting the language do all the work; you still need to play intentions just as strongly as with any other play.) Actors need to find the subtext to the lines and the obstacles in their paths. In most respects they will approach the text the same way, but with adjustments made to speaking and moving, and even these are easy adjustments to make with class work and practice. In *Playing Shakespeare*, John Barton, arguably the best living teacher of Shakespearean acting, says, "There is no basic difference between approaching a character when he plays Shakespeare and when he plays any other author, ancient or modern."

One of the interesting things about playing Shakespeare in

America is our sense of style in playing him. This is not a problem for the British actors, who are more formally trained and raised on Shakespeare from the womb. For American actors, who like to get down and dirty and are heavily influenced by film, it's an adjustment. And if you're wondering if you need to do a British dialect when acting Shakespeare, the answer is a resounding *no!*

If you're new to Shakespeare, I would encourage a simple three-step process: **understand, own, and sing.**

To **understand** means, first of all, to understand the text. What's being said? What do the words mean? What are the puns? What are the double entendres? What's going on with the character that he/she would choose these particular words at this particular moment?

But "to understand" also means to understand the time in which Shakespeare was writing. It means to be knowledgeable about the clothes, the customs, the eating habits, the music. All of these factors will greatly determine how you as an actor behave, as well as providing even more insight to the text.

Owning is the next step. It's not enough simply to understand what's going on, because that implies the information remains solely in the brain. That knowledge needs to come through in the acting, in the behavior. Owning means to own the text, own the physicality, own the character just as much as you would own those elements of a contemporary script. Actors generally have little problem owning the language from a Mamet or a Shepard play, and their relationship to Shakespeare should be similarly proprietary. Own the words! Make them your very own! Own the costumes, as if these were the clothes you wore on a daily basis. Own the stage movements, as if it were commonplace for you to pull out your rapier when an argument broke out. Don't let yourself get caught "acting" these elements. Own them.

The final step is **singing,** by which I don't mean *singing* singing, of course. I mean **singing.** Let me explain. Shakespeare's language is arguably the greatest ever written. His wordplay, his imagery, his sense of rhythm (and occasionally rhyme), his utter genius at articulating beautifully what we have all felt but lack the words to write, all combine to make his plays masterpieces of text. One of the common mistakes for young actors, then, is they stop at the owning process. They understand, they own, but they own in a contemporary fashion. Shakespeare's language needs to be owned, but it also needs to be sung. In other words, it's too good to be mumbled and stuttered through, common acting characteristics for contemporary plays.

I'm not saying it has to be something so "grand" and dramatic that it becomes false or ludicrous. Far from it. But I am saying that it is heightened language, and the beauty of it will emerge only if it is treated as heightened language. Someone once said that Shakespeare's words are like a bird, and for them to be happiest, you need to let them fly. In other words, don't keep them cooped up in the constraints of modern day speech.

Of all the lessons, this one requires the most outside work. Read and see as many of Shakespeare's plays as you can, and read the great Shakespearean acting books. Work on Shakespeare in class, in performance, on your own. It may not come easily, but it will come.

One thing that should give all actors hope is that this country is still looking for an American style for playing Shakespeare, something that is uniquely ours without being a pale copy of the British system. I encourage all actors to embrace Shakespeare and find their own way of bringing it alive. Don't fear Shakespeare. On the contrary, find your own way of bringing him to life. That's where the glory lies.

Lesson 95:
Get Rid of the Voice

You know what voice I mean. The little critic. The one who never shuts up. The one who floats around in your head and says, "You're not any good." "You'll never make it." "You're not good-looking enough to succeed." "You didn't deserve this part."

You know that voice.

I'm here to tell you two things: (1) we *all* have that voice in our heads, so you're definitely not alone, and (2) it's imperative that you shut that voice up.

There is nothing more defeating than negativity. It can zap the energy and confidence from the best of us if we're not careful, whether it's someone else's negativity or, worse, our own. The voice paralyzes us. It makes us doubt. It strips us of our confidence. It makes us tentative on-stage. It makes us second-guess. It makes it hard to commit and follow through. A simple imaginary voice does all of this; in fact, it can do more damage than all the critics combined.

So how do you silence this voice? Refuse to listen to it. It's there, and will always be there, so just accept that. Laugh at it, even. But don't let yourself listen to it. It won't do you any good, and you'll certainly never learn anything from the voice. So just ignore it. It's that simple.

If you get in the habit *now* of not listening to it, you'll be in much better shape as time goes on. I encourage you, from this point on, from this very minute on, refuse to listen to the voice. You'll be surprised how much more confident you will feel, both in life and on-stage.

Lesson 96:
Suffer for Your Art

Must all actors suffer? There's an easy answer to this, and it's, "yes." If you're an actor, you must suffer. You must also experience intense joy, sadness, exultation, relief, shame, pain, jubilation, embarrassment ... in short, every emotion known to man. Having said that, there's no reason to single out suffering any more than the other emotions.

The truth is, all actors — if they want to have any range at all and be able to tackle any type of character — must experience life to the fullest. That not only means trying and learning about new things, it also means keeping yourself open to the events around you, to the world around you, so that you are a human being who is affected by the life around you. If not, what will you possibly draw on for your characters?

One of the great ironies of many college "training programs" is that they shelter students from the rest of college and its offerings and a life outside the theatre. I'll tell you a secret in case you don't already know it: There is life outside the theatre, and it's your responsibility to soak it up. That means the good things and the bad. And sometimes that means suffering.

Lesson 97:
The Fab Five

Now that we're near the end of these lessons, I want to share with you what I believe are the five essential qualities all actors need to possess (in varying degrees) if they want to be successful.

Five qualities. That's all.

For an actor to be successful, this is what he or she needs to possess. Are you ready? Are you sitting down? You might want to highlight these. Here they are:

Talent.

Ambition.

Luck.

Look.

Knowledge.

Every actor needs some of these five elements to succeed. Let me say that again because I think it's important. Every actor needs *some* of these five elements to succeed. Each actor is blessed with a different ratio of these five elements, which, added up, create their "net worth" for getting cast. Some actors are rich in all five, some just in one. But to be successful in this business, you don't necessarily need to be strong in each, just strong in some.

Let me define and explain.

Talent: This is an easy one to understand. Some acting teachers claim you either have it or you don't. Some say just the opposite, that it can be taught. I won't bother entering into the nature vs. nurture debate, but as a prerequisite for getting cast, talent is the most highly rated. Granted, you may turn on the TV and claim not to see any talent there, and in some cases you may be right, but for an actor to continue working, there probably is at least *some* talent. How do you acquire talent? Through performances, classes, scene study, maybe even reading a book such as this one. In other words, work. Hands-on, on-your-feet work. Most successful actors are born with some native talent, but it all depends on what you do with that native talent that determines how successful you'll be. In other words, how hard you're willing to work and shape that talent is the crucial factor.

Ambition: You've heard and read the statistics about this business. Let's face it, the odds are against you. If only fifteen percent of the actors in the Screen Actors Guild (and we're not talking about the tens of thousands of actors who *want* to get in the Screen Actors Guild but can't) make $15,000 or more a year, it's pretty clear this is not the business to go into if you're planning on striking it rich. If half of all the professional actors in this country make a living wage below the poverty line in any given year, it's obvious this is one tough career choice. The people who succeed in this business are the ones who persevere, who believe in themselves, never stop working to improve themselves, and never stop fighting for roles. As author Erica Jong wrote, "Everyone has a talent; what is rare is the courage to follow that talent to the dark place where it leads." In this business, it's not enough to be a good actor; you have to be ambitious enough to fight against the odds. (By the way, if the word "ambition" rubs you the wrong way, you can use your own word. *Persistence* is good. So is *perseverance*. *Desire* isn't bad.) The important thing is the acknowledgment that if you're going to make it, you need to fight for yourself. And fight like hell.

Luck: I'm sorry, but even the most talented actor has, at some point in his or her life, been blessed with a lucky break. There are too many good actors out there, many of whom don't work consistently, and everyone needs to have some luck. It can be meeting an influential producer when you're doing your day job. Or being discovered at Schwab's Drug Store. Or getting accepted to a good graduate school, even though your slot could have been given to dozens of other qualified applicants. If this is depressing to you, it shouldn't be. Remember, most people make their luck. By getting out there and doing it — taking classes, attending theatre, auditioning, not being afraid to talk to people — you put yourself in a position to be "lucky."

Look: Everyone has a look; everyone is a certain type. Remember that. But the actors who are most successful are those who have correctly identified their look and have marketed themselves accordingly. True, it doesn't hurt if you're drop-dead gorgeous, but even that won't help you if you can't acknowledge you're drop-dead gorgeous. Perhaps the converse is more often true. There are so many actors out there who want to be leading men and women, and yet they should more correctly think of themselves as character actors and start developing skills appropriate for a character actor (comic skills, for example). Again, the question is not whether you have a look or not (you do!); the question is whether you can truly recognize your look and play it for all it's worth.

Knowledge: All the acting wisdom in the world won't make you a successful actor, but the more you understand about acting, and, perhaps more importantly, the more you understand about *the business* of acting, the more you increase your chances of working. It's not that you need to know everything about the business, but you do need to know enough so you won't continually be shooting yourself in the foot. So, for example, when you step into a commercial audition and the casting director says, "Slate," you know what they're talking about. So when you go to a network for a new pilot you know how to behave and whether or not to hold your script. So when you show up on the set for your first film you know what to expect when the director calls in Second Team. Anything that can help you succeed as an actor (in an audition, in front of a camera, on the stage) can only help your chances of working, and working again.

Those are the five elements. Do you need significant depth in each? Not necessarily. Are there some elements that are more important than others? Sure, talent is a good one, but with TV and film, your look is important too.

So how does it work, combining these five qualities? Let's take, as an example, the cast of *Baywatch*. These maybe weren't the best actors in the business, and it might be fair to say that their talent wasn't as strong as many other actors found on television (*The West Wing, The Sopranos, Frasier*), but they possessed other qualities instead. Number one, they understood their *look*. They knew they were hunks and hard-bodies and marketed themselves accordingly. Good for them. That alone proves they had *knowledge* enough to understand their strengths and weaknesses. They were probably *ambitious* enough to get on that show; after all, if you've ever spent any time in Los Angeles, you know there's no shortage of people with good bodies. And, lastly, they probably had some *luck* along the way that helped them get noticed. So even though their talent quotient might have been low, they compensated in other categories. And you know what? They were on one of the highest rated syndicated television shows in history, and made a great deal of money in the process. While it might be easy to bash them, especially in terms of their talent, I say more power to them. They understood their strengths and played accordingly. We should all be so smart. And what good would it be for us to judge them? Such a comparison would do us no good. As long as they're happy with what they're doing, that's the important thing.

The important thing for each actor is to continually assess their strengths and weaknesses in the Fab Five categories and strive always to improve what needs improving. Again, the stronger you are in each category, the more you increase your chances of working. It's that simple.

Lesson 98:
If You Want It, Work For It

Okay. So you want to be an actor. You want to work consistently. You want to have a career in theatre (or film or TV). Fine. Then you need to work for it. Don't just talk about it; work for it.

How, you ask? Simple.

Take classes. Do research. Get the best headshot possible. Update your résumé. Lift weights. Send out mailings. Do showcases. Find friends who can give you honest feedback. Get involved with a theatre company. Keep an audition journal. Read every play you can get your hands on. Attend every production you can afford. Audition like crazy. Do student films. Keep in shape. Take dance classes. Get a good haircut. Meet other actors. Jog. Work on monologs. Do your homework. Go to grad school. Avoid friends who are bitter about their own lack of a career. Write an actor's credo — a statement of what you expect from yourself in the theatre — and post it above your desk, your bed, on your website. Remind yourself daily of what you expect, not from others, but from yourself.

You want more ideas? Okay. Write. Make sure your day job doesn't interfere with auditions. Do summer stock. Swim. Get a hobby. Read all of Shakespeare's plays. Avoid friends who complain that's it just a business and there is no art. (It *is* a business; now get over it.) Study the great films. Add to your audition portfolio. Find peace where and when you can. Do play readings with a group of friends. Memorize the great Shakespearean monologs. When you get cast, learn your lines quickly. Understand yourself. Confront your fears. Put together a showcase. Write a one-person play. Do standup comedy. *But.* And here's the catch. Don't create these things to move up the ladder, to get the agent, to be seen. Do these things because you need to, because you're an actor, and actors need to express or else they'll burst.

Expand your intellectual horizons. The great Sarah Bernhardt wrote, "the actor must be — if not a scholar or a learned man — at least what used to be called 'an all-round man,' that is, he should not be inferior in the matter of acquired knowledge to the average of mankind." In other words, read the classics. Devour the Sunday *New York Times*. Get a subscription to *The New Yorker*. Read news magazines religiously.

And that's not all. Visit museums. Attend concerts. Learn a dialect. Go to the gym. Get in shape. Get a pet. Engage yourself in a committed relationship. Spend time outside. Learn to fish (hike, climb, skate, ski). Don't shy away from physical labor. Keep a journal. Articulate your thoughts, desires, hopes. Stay away from green rooms. Stop telling theatre stories. Experience life outside of the theatre. Don't give up.

Will it be easy? No. Will there be obstacles? Yes, hundreds. Will you consider changing professions? Nearly every day.

But if you want it, keep working for it, and don't let those obstacles stand in your way. You know your purpose, you know what you want, so pursue it, and pursue it with great calmness and determination.

If you want to hear it from the poet's mouth, turn to Longfellow:

"The heights by great men reached and kept

Were not attained by sudden flight,

But they, while their companions slept,

Were toiling upward in the night."

There is no substitute for hard work and perseverance, no substitute for "toiling upward in the night." As the old saying goes, "Success is 1% inspiration and 99% perspiration."

So if you want it, work for it.

Simple, yes?

Lesson 99:
Don't Get Too Comfortable

Let's say you take these lessons to heart. Let's say you dedicate yourself to the craft of acting and that all your hard work pays off: you're getting cast on a consistent basis. Whatever level you're at — college, grad school, community theatre, professional actor in theatre, film, or TV — you're suddenly working on a consistent basis.

First of all, congratulations! I mean it. I know that not all of these lessons are easy, and all of them involve some serious work. Congratulations on identifying your weaknesses and working on them.

Now a word of warning: Don't get too comfortable. There is nothing more discouraging than watching an artist in any field settle back and get content. From that point on they cease to create anything original or of real value. Instead of being hungry, instead of pushing themselves, they get complacent. They get content. They begin to settle.

"Oh, I don't really need to figure out my character's objectives," they say. Or, "I'll just use the personalizations I used with my previous character." Or, "Now that I've made it, I can just kick back. I've already proved I'm a good actor, so why bother pushing myself?"

These are the satanic lessons, the polar opposite of what you've been reading here. Yes, it's true you should enjoy your victories, but that doesn't mean not doing any more work. Acting, like any art, is a lifelong profession. You continue to grow and change, and your work needs to reflect those changes. This next character you'll be playing is no doubt different from the previous; make sure you play it that way. As you improve as an actor, you'll discover you have new weaknesses. Address those. Now that you've mastered your previous weaknesses, you'll have time to conquer these new ones.

Above all, stay hungry. Stay interested. Stay motivated. Yes, be pleased with your progress, but not to the point of getting comfortable and settling back. It's the actor who doesn't let himself get complacent who remains the most interesting to watch.

Lesson 100:
Do the Work, Enjoy the Victories

It would be a shame if you were to finish this book and think there were no reward for all your efforts, that a life of acting is a life of drudgery and meaningless toil. Far from it. I challenge anyone to match the highs that come from a successful life as an actor with the highs from any other profession. I just can't imagine it can be done. Sure, Michael Jordan hitting a game-winning shot in the NBA Finals is pretty good. And I'll admit Serena Williams winning Wimbledon in consecutive years must feel pretty nice. But you know from experience the highs that come from being on-stage when things are clicking: when you're either making the audience laugh or you're making them cry or you're dazzling them with your singing or your dancing or your prowess with Shakespearean speech. Those are some of the highest highs that can be experienced.

And actors are lucky. They get a curtain call afterwards for the audience to express their appreciation. Talk about sweet. How many professions can claim a curtain call at the end of their day's work? My brother's a computer programmer. He likes what he does, and he's great at his job, but he sure doesn't get a curtain call every day. Actors do.

When you do the work and things fall into place, yes, you should enjoy that progress. You should savor that success. You should feel good about yourself and the accomplishments you've made, because what you've done is something only a small percentage of people do: get on-stage and effectively portray a character to an audience's delight. You will be so admired for your skills, and you should accept that. Enjoy it.

And if you're like the majority of actors, you should enjoy it all the more because you've had to work very hard to achieve it. There are few actors out there who are complete "naturals." The rest have to put themselves through the paces, they have to absorb the lessons of acting, they have to pay dues before they can begin to find success. Good. That makes success all the sweeter when it happens.

So yes, do the work.

And yes, please enjoy those victories.

Epilogue: A Call to Arms

John F. Kennedy was fond of quoting Luke 12:48, "To whom much is given, much is required." As artists with an ability to act, you have one of the greatest gifts in the world. Now use that gift responsibly.

Actors, take matters into your own hands. Don't wait for the indifferent machine to hire you or not hire you. Don't let yourself be the pawn, accepting the producer's scraps from the table of "entertainment." Demand work that makes a difference. Hold yourselves to the highest possible standard. While it's true that, by contrast, a writer doesn't need to be hired to write, she can write any time, and while it's equally true that an actor must audition and then be cast before having a chance to ply his trade, an actor can still exercise his skills.

How, you ask?

Don't let yourself get stuck doing just what you're told. You're an actor, for heaven's sake. Make interesting choices. Use your creative juices to create roles that are dynamic, winning, original, *engaging*.

Stay busy. Put into practice the ideas from **Lesson 99**. *Master your craft.*

Regain your self-respect.

Hide the work.

Don't try to please.

Honor impulses.

Be hungry.

Resist slick.

Have heart.

Talk.

Listen.

Engage.

Allow freedom.

Do the work; enjoy the victories.

Laugh often and much.

As Albert Einstein wrote, "Try not to become a person of success, but rather try to become a person of value."

It's time for actors to take back the theatre, to rescue it from the stultifying, passionless *machine* it has often become.

It is your choice.

It is your responsibility.

No pressure, but the future of the theatre rests with you.

"I am certain that after the dust of centuries has passed over our cities," John Kennedy once wrote, "we too will be remembered not for victories or defeats in battle or in politics, but for our contribution to the human spirit."

That's what a true actor brings to the world: a contribution to the human spirit.

Good luck. And break legs.

Recommended Reading

Ackerman, Diane. *A Natural History of the Senses*. Knopf Publishing Group, New York, 1991.

Adler, Stella. *The Technique of Acting*. Bantam Books, New York, 1990.

Ahart, John. *The Director's Eye*. Meriwether Publishing Ltd., Colorado Springs, CO, 2001.

Barton, John. *Playing Shakespeare*. Methuen Drama, London, 2001.

Boleslavsky, Richard. *Acting — the First Six Lessons*. Theater Arts Book, New York, 1991.

Brestoff, Richard. *The Great Acting Teachers and Their Methods*. Smith and Kraus, Inc., Lyme, NH, 1996.

Brook, Peter. *The Empty Space*. Touchstone Books, New York, 1995.

Brook, Peter. *Evoking (And Forgetting!) Shakespeare*. Theatre Communications Group, New York, 2003.

Bruder, Melissa, et. al. *A Practical Handbook for the Actor*. Knopf Publishing Group, New York, 1986.

Cohen, Robert. *Acting Professionally*. Sixth Edition, McGraw-Hill, New York, 2003.

Cole, Toby and Helen Krich Chinoy, editors. *Actors on Acting*. Fourth Edition, Crown Publishing Group, New York, 1995.

Corredor, J. Ma. *Conversations with Casals*. E. P. Dutton & Co., Inc., New York, 1957.

Hagen, Uta. *Respect for Acting*. Macmillan Publishing Company, New York, 1991.

Hull, S. Loraine. *Strasberg's Method*. Ox Bow Press, Connecticut, 1987.

Johnstone, Keith. *Impro*. Taylor and Francis, Inc., New York, 1987.

Jory, Jon. *Tips*. Smith and Kraus, Inc., Lyme, NH, 2000.

Lewis, Robert. *Method — or Madness?* Samuel French, Inc., New York, 1958.

Linklater, Kristin. *Freeing the Natural Voice*. Quite Specific Media Group, Ltd., 1978.

Mamet, David. *True and False*. Random House, Inc., New York, 1999.

Meisner, Sanford and Dennis Longwell. *Sanford Meisner on Acting*. Random House, Inc., New York, 1987.

Olivier, Laurence. *On Acting*. Simon and Schuster, New York, 1986.

Shurtleff, Michael. *Audition*. Bantam, New York, 1979.

Spolin, Viola. *Improvisation for the Theater*. Third Edition, Northwestern University Press, 1999.

Stanislavski, Constantine. *An Actor Prepares*. Translated Elizabeth R. Hapgood, Routledge/Theater Arts Books, New York, 1936.

Stanislavski, Constantine. *Building a Character*. Translated Elizabeth R. Hapgood, Theater Arts Books, New York, 1949.

Stanislavski, Constantine. *Creating a Role*. Translated Elizabeth R. Hapgood, Theater Arts Books, New York, 1961.

About the Author

A graduate of the Yale School of Drama and the University of Illinois, Tom Isbell spent his professional career acting in theatre, film, and TV, working opposite Robert DeNiro, Ed Harris, Helen Hunt, Lynn Redgrave, Rosemary Harris, Hal Holbrook, Anne Bancroft, Sarah Jessica Parker, John Turturro, Angela Bassett, and others. TV credits include *Designing Women*, *L.A. Law*, *Golden Girls*, *Murder She Wrote*, *Coach*, *Family Ties*, *Columbo*, and recurring roles on *Jake and the Fat Man* and *Sisters*. Film credits include *84 Charing Cross Road*, *Jacknife*, *Clear and Present Danger*, *The Abyss*, and *True Lies*. He was also the subject of a PBS documentary, *Starting in Innocence*.

He has written and performed three one-person plays, including *Me & JFK*, which has been produced in New York, Los Angeles, and Egypt. With John Ahart, he co-authored *Walt Whitman and the Civil War*, which premiered at the Great American People Show in 1995.

As a director, Isbell has taken two productions to the Kennedy Center as part of the Kennedy Center American College Theater Festival (KCACTF): *Dear Finder*, a documentary play about the Holocaust, and *The Movie Game*, written by Adam Hummel. He is the former National Playwriting Program chair for Region V of KCACTF.

An associate professor at the University of Minnesota Duluth, he was recently named the Albert Tezla Scholar/Teacher of the Year, as well as a Horace T. Morse Distinguished Teacher, the highest undergraduate teaching honor given within the University of Minnesota. He is happily married to Pat Isbell, who is both an actress and elementary school teacher.

www.ingramcontent.com/pod-product-compliance
Lightning Source LLC
Chambersburg PA
CBHW071852090426
42811CB00004B/577